EGG BANJO AROUND TH.

A COLLECTION OF GUNNER ANECDOTES.

Edited by
DUNCAN SMITH

ROYALTIES TO THE GUNNER HERITAGE APPEAL

© Copyright HOMESTEAD PUBLICATIONS 1995
West Cottage, Top Street, Pilton, Somerset
BA4 4DF

ISBN 0-952-43230-7

British Library Cataloguing in Publication Data.
A catalogue record for this book is available from the
British Library.

All rights reserved. No part of this publication may be
reproduced, stored in a retrieval system, or transmitted in
any form or by any means, electronic, mechanical,
photocopying, recording or otherwise without prior
permission from HOMESTEAD PUBLICATIONS.
So there !!

Printed in Great Britain by PRINTCRAFT

DUNCAN SMITH

After a relatively brief spell in the Royal Regiment he completed his commission in 7 Para RHA and is now a teacher. He lives in Somerset with Rachel and their dog Millie.

OPENING GAMBIT
8th May, 1995

One of the first lessons learned by Gunners is that *Ubique* means everywhere. Second - and no doubt equally important - comes the news that no good troop of Gunners runs out of bread and eggs, the basic ingredients for an 'Egg Banjo'. Rightly then, "Egg Banjos From around the World" records for posterity the tales of Gunners who have served - quite literally - all over the place. A sincere thanks is extended to all contributors; to Rachel for her tolerance; to Dicky Haldenby and Peter Bates for their support throughout and to the Regiment for its backing. I hope most - if not all - of the stories which grace the pages will strike a chord with all linked to the Gunners - and perhaps raise a smile.

Happy reading,

FOREWORD

Major General C G Cornock CB MBE
Honorary Colonel
7th Parachute Regiment,
Royal Horse Artillery

As someone who survived a few tours in Northern Ireland on egg banjos straight from the cookhouse in the early hours of the morning, I simply could not resist the invitation to write this foreword for a fellow Airborne Gunner.

British soldiers of all ages should be grateful to Duncan Smith for taking the time and care to assemble so many anecdotes. The range of the contributions is immense and therefore there is something for everyone. Each story brings out the wonderful humour which servicemen enjoy and which makes the awful times more bearable. Above all his book highlights the greatest and essential feature of soldiering - it must be fun.

I hope you will enjoy reading the tales as much as I did and that the marvellous memories of being a soldier will flood back wherever you are serving or have served.

CONTRIBUTORS

Lieutenant-Colonel J G Barber-Lomax CBE TD RA(Retd) - Harpenden.
Lieutenant-Colonel F Blofield RA(Retd) - Dyfed.
G Blatchford Esq - Highcliffe-on-Sea.
K Bortkiewicz Esq BA - Polish Anti-Aircraft Association - London.
R Brooks Esq - RAA Woolwich & Plumstead Branch.
L W Brown Esq - Southampton.
J W H Cockhill Esq - Southsea.
T S Cox Esq - London.
M G D'Arcy Esq - Devon.
R Duck Esq - London.
F R E Durrie Esq - Argyll.
V Ellender Esq - Kessingland.
General Sir Martin Farndale KCB. Master Gunner, St James' Park.
W Francis Esq - Leeds.
Rev G W Glew(Hon CF) - Canterbury.
Colonel G S Hatch CBE - Woolwich.
Lieutenant-Colonel H W Hawkins TD - Liverpool.
P Head Esq - Richmond.
S Hutson Esq - Lincoln.
J Ince Esq - Ontario, Canada.
Major G Jacobs MBE RA(Retd) - Bickton.
M L James Esq BEM - Maritime RA Old Comrades' Association, Isle of Wight.
A Jenkins Esq - Portsmouth.
W J Meredith Esq - Swansea.
Lieutenant-General Sir Douglas Packard - Lower Ufford.
W J Page Esq - Portsmouth.
H J Porter Esq - Co Antrim.
Brigadier S P Roberston MBE TD JP DL - Orkney.
Mrs V Robinson - Fillongley.
Sir Harry Secombe CBE - London.
Major F S G Shore MC CdeG - Long Ashton.
D I A Smith Esq - Wickham.
R Thomas Esq - Lee-on-Solent.
General Sir Harry Tuzo GCB OBE MC DL MA - Fakenham.
P Viggers Esq MP - Westminster/Gosport.
Colonel D Walton CBE TD MA - Matlock.

EGG BANJOS FROM AROUND THE WORLD

A COLLECTION OF GUNNER ANECDOTES.

Lieutenant-Colonel J G Barber-Lomax CBE TD RA(Retd) - Harpenden.

A DANGEROUS WEEKEND AT KUT!

In 1942, I was a Gunner Staff Officer in Persia enjoying the delights of meteor telegrams, airburst ranging and clinometers. However, my lifestyle was soon set for an upheaval when, with the arrival of a wire one morning, I was posted to Baghdad.

The posting order to join the Quartermaster General's Branch at the newly formed GHQ Persia and Iraq Command marked the start of three years' pressing work assisting the Aid to Russia programme prior-to and long-after Stalingrad. The work was very demanding but the periods of relaxation - when they did come - were often in very unusual circumstances.

On one particular occasion in the Autumn of 1943, I was detailed with two captains to attend the 'house-warming' of Sheik Mohammed of Kut who had recently moved into a new 'palace' and was desperate to celebrate with a few British officers. The invitation instructed us to come armed with our own personal weapons to enable us to participate more fully in the 'fun and games' of such gatherings. Remembering its evil reputation from the First World War, I was intrigued to know what I would find at Kut.

The journey from Baghdad lasted about two hours and jumping from the station wagon, each carrying a rifle and several clips of .303 ammo, the three of us were met by an Arabic-speaking District Officer who escorted us to our quarters.

Compared to my own room in the Mess, my accommodation for the visit was luxury! A single bed with sheets and coverlet, a carpet and, wonder-of-wonders a washbasin with running water - hot and cold.

At the time there was a worldwide shortage of shipping, so quite how these furnishings from Harrods had got there was a mystery. But got there they had - along with the highly-polished walnut table and good quality dinner service which greeted us later that evening as we dined with the Emir in his dining room. The following morning - after toast, Oxford marmalade and - rather inevitably - a boiled egg, we were taken to a small island in the River Tigris where the promised 'fun and games' was to commence. Part of the island was devoid of vegetation and, in contrast, the other was covered in scrub up to six feet high in places. The motley crew of locals who met us and the other invited guests on our arrival were friendly enough but looked decidedly menacing brandishing various pots and pans. A closer study revealed that some were in fact carrying an array of antiquated firearms rather similar to flintlocks and I remember feeling as the 'fun and games' were explained that from this scene of apparent tranquillity, a perilously dangerous predicament could materialise.

We, the guests were expected to advance up the scrub part of the island and the locals - a short way behind - were expected to bang and clash their various cooking and shooting implements to scare any pig which might be lumbering to our front. Any beast which decided to take flight from this advancing racket would - in theory at least - end the day on a spit roast with a single .303 round somewhere within its hide.

In principle, this was a straightforward exercise but with the scrub being so dense in places, shooters and beaters very quickly became invisible to one another. Application of even basic fields of fire was virtually impossible and being the only Major present, I decided to take charge of this potentially lethal scenario. It was arranged that the guests would advance slowly forward and - when the scrubland became dangerously dense - I would blow my whistle. On hearing the whistle, all rifles were to be held aloft so that no shots could be fired until I deemed it sufficiently safe to recommence the shoot.

Our advance was painfully slow. I was becoming increasingly apprehensive about these 'fun and games': how ferocious were these wild pigs which lay somewhere to our front and more worryingly perhaps, how trustworthy were the more lethally-armed beaters to our rear? The more ground this shooting party covered, the more apprehensive I became. With every shot which occasionally reverberated through the scrub, the more my pulse quickened. Then suddenly, immediately to my front I heard it.

The scrub before me rustled. Small saplings fell flat to the ground and to my utter dismay I saw a very large, very angry pig charging directly at me. Somehow, the beast-possessed swerved to avoid me but after the morning's anxiety something inside took control of my senses. There was no way this creature was going to get away. As the rapidly-disappearing rump sped into the scrubland, I sank to one knee and with a deftness not displayed since my days at OTC many years' previous, proceeded to empty a whole magazine into the rear-end of the unfortunate hulk. Never mind the lot of the poor beast - the relief I experienced from this release of pent-up apprehension was unbeatable and well-earned. So much for the pinpoint accuracy normally demanded of a marksman going in for his kill.

It had hardly been a morning of fun and games and when we stopped for our picnic lunch where we once again experienced the luxurious lifestyle of a Sheik - a chicken breast each AND a bottle of McEwans beer - our return to GHQ could not come soon enough.

Lt-Col F Blofield RA(Retd) Dyfed

THE CROMWELL CATCH

In the summer of 1940, I was a newly-joined recruit at the 12th Field Training Regiment in Bordon Camp - just 19 and just out of school. With the German invasion expected any moment we waited anxiously - poised to deter any fifth columnists from signalling to the invading hordes.

Unknown to the lowly Gunner, the codeword given to offset an enemy advance was CROMWELL. On being issued, our orders were simply to "Get-fell-in" on the Square with rifle (no ammo), wearing full marching order and await further instructions.

One day - as I think is well-known now - CROMWELL was given in error and the order to respond to the pending crisis was duly barked-up to us. It was an instruction more horrifying than any invasion! Not only were we uncertain how to assemble our kit but it would mean having to discard the pieces of wood we had just made to keep it square on the locker - surely not! Worse still, what would happen if it got dirty for the next day's barrack room inspection? The consequences were unthinkable.

We made our way to the Square where I was given a small metal object with orders to go up the clock tower in the centre of the barracks and locate any unsuspecting fifth columnists. Clearly a responsible task, I and two of my companions headed for the hatch in the ceiling of the tower - and up I went. I was pretty slim in those days, but with rifle and big pack - which no one had told me I could remove - I got stuck.

After much humping, grumping and grimacing, my companions finally managed to shove me through the opening for the start of a very, very uncomfortable night spent praying that no fifth columnists would emerge. Things were at least worrying and at worst devastatingly perilous. And someh-

throughout my trauma, the nation slept.

My situation looked untenable. I had no idea how to find the fifth columnists using the brand new boxlike thing issued freshly from the stores and to compound my predicament, I had no idea how to open the thing - if open it did. At that stage in my military career all I had learned from the army was rudimentary; if I damaged the wretched thing, I would certainly be invited to pay for it when Hitler finally received his comeuppance!

The night passed - eventually - but it was some three months later at OCTU that the enigma of the night in the clock tower finally made some sort of sense. I had been issued with a prismatic compass!

✥ ✥ ✥ ✥ ✥ ✥

G Blatchford Esq – Highcliffe-on-Sea.

CONTINENTAL BREAKFAST

For two days, our Number 5 gun had been idling in a field somewhere in France awaiting further orders to advance. Rightly, the gun crew were really making the most of this lull in hostilities - the new orders could come anytime - within the hour or sometime next week.

The sausages were doing nicely on the Number 3 cooker and in all honesty, there really was nothing handy in the way of side arms when a visitor joined their throng.

Dressed in field grey, he had come from a nearby tree - sort of dropped-in – you might say. The odd thing was they all knew he was there but to a man each avoided eye contact. The thought of hitting him over the head with the frying pan was considered but was dismissed by one Gun Number who felt the best way out of the situation was to offer the miserable looking fellow a fag. Entente Cordial had been strengthened further by the time the Jerry sniper was handed-over to the Red Caps. It seems the common liking for sausages had served to bring captive and captors together - they departed each others' company on first name terms!

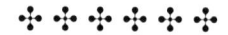

✤ ✤ ✤ ✤ ✤ ✤

K Bortkiewicz Esq BA – Polish Anti Aircraft Association, London.
Gunner Bortkiewicz
8th Polish Heavy AA Artillery Regiment
Italy, Summer 1944.

MADNESS AT MADONNA

The Germans were withdrawing briskly on the Adriatic Front with the 2nd Polish Corps in hot pursuit (there's no accounting for taste!) These joyfully friendly proceedings were being impeded by us as we crawled along at the dignified speed of only 7 miles an hour - (our radar was more sensitive to a jolt than a primadonna to a slight!). Behind us, the keen types were getting impatient and becoming concerned that they may lose touch with the Germans.

As expected and as had happened a few days earlier, we were unceremoniously ordered off the road in Madonna - a suburb of Pescara. Quickly the Regiment settled into its new - albeit temporary - surroundings and our troop chose to bivouac in the grounds of a rather pretty palace. Sadly, Wlasow's cossacks and their horses had left the place in a filthy condition, but the area offered outstanding views over the busy town and in the harbour below, a Royal Navy minesweeper was busy harvesting the explosive crop left by the fleeing Germans.

With little to occupy our time, two drivers and I decided to undertake a spot of useful reconnaissance and began to explore the area. About half a kilometre inland, the ground rose steeply forming an escarpment and beyond that it was fairly flat with a smattering of farmhouses. Moving from house to house we searched for somewhere to buy eggs and, with the Italians at this point on our side, for any free wine which might come our way.

Edging ourselves towards the edge of the escarpment, we found a gun emplacement set in a concrete revetment. There was an old 3-inch high angle gun with quarters for the crew and stores built underground. In an instant, one of the drivers suggested that being a Gunner, I would have the know-how to drop a few of the shells into the sea. How could anyone resist such flattery?

From somewhere in the annals of my mind I produced the well-versed theory that by standing as we were at the sea edge....and with the horizon 6 miles away..... and with a barrel this size (it was big!)..... and being situated some meters above sea level....yes, there was a good chance of seeing the shell-burst. So, ramming a shell into the breech and loading the charge and percussion cap (it was that type of gun), I attached a piece of telephone wire to the firing lever and lead the other end into the shelters.

In my best gun drill manner I took command of the position:
"Elevation 45'"
"Direction...thataway!...no-no you idiot...the other way!"
"Take shelter....FIRE!!"

The gun roared. We rushed out from our shelter just in time to see a fountain of water rise and fall in the wake of the minesweeper. I assume her crew must have been closed-up as they automatically responded with an AA barrage to repel what surely must have been an air attack.

Now, at this point, intelligent lads would have skedaddled, but alas, not so we! Goaded by my crew's previous remarks about my knowledge of gunnery, I started to inspect the barrel with an assumed understanding of all things technical, however, this supposed technical inspection was suddenly interrupted by a Polish voice. "Hands up! Don't move!"

It was the familiar voice of the usually very genial Sergeant Skudlarek who was leading an armed patrol from the troop bivouac site. He was somewhat less friendly now and ordering us to keep our mouths shut but allowing us at least to lower our hands, he marched us to the Troop HQ.

Lieutenant Rachwalski – the Troop Commander was a well-read man and most definitely had a lively imagination. His proposals for a suitable punishment would have made Dante green with envy. His mind was clearly working over-time and he was surpassing even himself with the range of suitable options available to meet the severity of our crime, when he was interrupted by the roar of a motorcycle.

The despatch rider from RHQ squealed to a halt and handing our commander a signal, yelled at the top of his voice, "Most urgent!"

The Troop had been tasked to send out a strong Recce Patrol and in the true spirit of army delegation, the Troop Commander handed the message to his second-in-command before vanishing in the general direction of the Troop office.

Looking markedly at me, Second Lieutenant Ostoja-Steblecki bellowed, "I want volunteers!" I was there like a shot: the most prompt volunteer of the entire Italian campaign.

The patrol went out, the Troop rejoined the front line, the 2nd Polish Corps captured Ancona and the Regiment was deployed to defend its port. With such activity, my episode with the gun emplacement was never mentioned again!

✢ ✢ ✢ ✢ ✢ ✢

R Brooks Esq - President RAA Woolwich and Plumstead Branch
258 Battery
65th Field Regiment RA
44th Division Alamein,
October 1942.

COUNTDOWN CALAMITY AT ALAMEIN

In the days prior to Alamein, I was assistant Gun Position Officer. We had been firing mainly concentration and counter-battery shoots and on the 21st of October we were given the particulars for a Corps target which we would be shooting later in the day. With the details recorded, my job in the Command Post was over for the time being and so all I had to do now was give the troop the order to FIRE!

It was a very hot afternoon and with a short while to go, I sat musing on the edge of the well dug-in Command Post - megaphone in hand. With the minutes ticking away, the wireless operator broke the relative silence saying, "30 seconds to go. 20, 30, 10, 5, 4, 3...". As the countdown ended, I picked-up my megaphone and gave the order - FIRE!

To my complete amazement and abject horror, instead of the whole area erupting as one would expect from a Corps shoot, the only guns to break the uneasy silence were my four 25-pounders. With the smell of cordite still hanging in the air, the telephone rang. A highly vexed CO was calling for blood.

"Who fired those b***** guns?"

A terrible sinking feeling pervaded and - with a croaking voice - I picked-up the handpiece and admitted my guilt. "It was me sir, I'm very sorry but I over-heard the signaller synchronizing his watch!"

EPILOGUE

It later transpired that the 'target' in question had been passed-on from our Intelligence people and was a meeting taking place between Rommel and his Generals! I fully expected to be court martialled for my faux pas, but with the battle joined in earnest a few days later, I escaped with an almighty rollocking!

✜ ✜ ✜ ✜ ✜ ✜

L W Brown Esq - Southampton.

THE TROUBLE WITH TEWTS

Tactical Exercises Without Troops (TEWTS) were very popular after war broke-out and I'll never forget one such imaginary exercise which I took part-in after being called-up from the TA in 1939.

Spending all day loading our imaginary ammunition into our imaginary gun, the Sergeant Number 1 and I were doing our best to play things for real. Comparatively speaking though, we had it easy. Somewhere else in the exercise area, somebody was busy imagining that a Royal Naval destroyer was a short distance out to sea providing a highly effective but - nonetheless - entirely invisible bombardment directed at an enemy stronghold.

At various times during the exercise, an umpire - an officer - would come up to my Sergeant and issue fire control orders which I duly carried-out. During one particularly intense period of firing, the umpire bellowed "Stop Firing!" Pausing as if allowing the smell of cordite to clear from his nostrils and the ringing of shell cases to cease, the umpire turned to my Sergeant saying: "Number 1, exactly where are you getting your ammunition from?" As ever, my Sergeant's timing was impeccable; "Same place as your destroyer,...Sir!"

✜ ✜ ✜ ✜ ✜ ✜

From the magazine "322 in Italy" dated 28th January 1946.

    Driver Roberts (our CO's Driver): *Was I really exceeding the speed limit?*
    American MP: *Brother, I ain't pinching you for exceeding the speed limit, I'm pinching you for flying too low!*

✠ ✠ ✠ ✠ ✠ ✠

J W H Cockhill Esq - Southsea – less than half a mile from his former 4.5 AA gun-pit on Southsea Common!

> "I'll be there, I'll be there
> In that little harness room behind the Square.
> When they're taking the horses to water
> I'll be kissing the Colonel's daughter
> In that little harness room behind the Square."
> Weybourne Summer Camp August 1939.

In 1938, our relationship with the Germans was - compared to the French (lots of garlic and very foreign) – fine. Boys on exchange visits came back with photos of themselves dressed in SS uniforms propped-up against plywood mock-up tanks. When the Germans got involved in the Spanish Civil War however, things cooled-off considerably. Those with communist leanings went off to join the International Brigade, but those of us with hard-earned jobs opted for the TA.

In late August, six of us - all junior clerks at High Street Banks – filed into the local drill hall and enlisted to assist with the air defence of the country, (we had seen a feature about it on the cinema news). Even as we took our oath, things were going seriously wrong. Having entered the wrong drill hall, we were in fact enlisting into a searchlight regiment of the Royal Engineers.

Realising our error, we somehow managed to escape from the Orderly Room and finding the correct drill hall, managed to enlist once again - twice in one night!

✣ ✣ ✣ ✣ ✣ ✣

Shortly after war was declared, some of us were given a night off. I went to see an Ian Hardy play at the Kings Theatre in Southsea and during the interval encountered a dilemma. Standing in the tiny cloakroom, I found myself between a Captain in the Royal Marines and a Lieutenant in the Royal Navy. Did one salute in such a confined space? If so, to whom did one direct the salute?...and even more worrying, which hand did one use - the right one was already occupied!

✣ ✣ ✣ ✣ ✣ ✣

It was shortly after Mareth that six of us were transferred to Infantry OCTU prior to the Italian landings. Being selected for the course was one thing, but getting there was an initiative test in itself. Given seven days' rations, we were told to find our own way back to base depot at Almaza - some 1000 miles away!

On arrival at 152 Transit Camp at Tripoli, it became our responsibility to escort POWs back to Alex in Liberty Ships. The ships had previously carried the flimsy two gallon petrol tins and not surprisingly - stank! Midway through the passage, a German feltwebel took one of the Italian rifles we had been issued and rather than turning it on us, promptly gave us our first lesson in stripping and assembling the thing. Before presenting arms and returning the weapon to its rightful owner however, he gave one more vital demonstration - how to load the wooden bullets which went with it...the African Campaign was indeed over!

✣ ✣ ✣ ✣ ✣ ✣

While serving as an officer in 14th RHA, we were joined by a new colonel. A jockey-sized figure with a monocle, he had won fame at the pre-war Royal Tournaments as a rider and swordsman. His favourite (and only) story was of the Larkhill Summer Ball when he chanced to comment on the whiteness and softness of a young lady's hands and arms. "That's because I always wear buckskin gloves", she said. "Damn me my girl", replied the diminutive officer, "I always wear buckskin breaches but my bum's as brown as a berry!".

✥ ✥ ✥ ✥ ✥ ✥

TS Cox Esq - London
10 Battery
17th Field Regiment RA

BRITISH - AND PROUD OF IT!

We were in action and the 15cwt wireless truck was up to its axles in mud. Quite rightly, the Gun Position Officer was in a filthy temper and flinging a wireless set into a jeep and taking with him another signaller, he told me to help the driver dig-out the truck and then follow-on later. We enlisted the help of an Italian farmer and his two oxen and before long the truck was free from the quagmire and we prepared to set off. But the farmer was having none of it. He refused to let us pass without payment for his toiling and that of his livestock. Reluctantly, we handed him some Lire, but still the farmer shook his head and indicated he wanted payment in cigarettes. There then followed an almighty row between the driver and the farmer which caused the driver - in a fit of rage to bellow – "B......Y FOREIGNERS".

This hardly served to quell the situation and when I ventured that it was perhaps we who were the foreigners – after all we were in Italy – he became even more irate. "Don't you EVER call me foreign – I'm British!". (Therein lies our attitude to the Common Market and Maarstricht – may the tunnel breed it out of us!).

✣ ✣ ✣ ✣ ✣ ✣

This one is such a perfect schoolboy howler, it's almost too good to be true! I was on duty with a fellow signaller in the Command Post when a message came in from one of our Observation Posts. My companion was - it has to be said - not the best of operators, in fact in all honesty he wasn't very good at all. When he transcribed the message, it came out as "..seen Russian Water Patrol..". This didn't strike a chord with anything I had heard before, so I offered to check it back for him. Sadly, he was a tiny fellow, about 5 feet-nothing tall and what he lacked in stature - like so many smaller people - he more than made up for in aggression. My offer of help was rejected and insisting that the message was in fact correct, he sent it off to the powers that be. Several hours later, as I half expected, we were asked to check the message back and what should it have been but, "..send rations, water, petrol..". I hate to say I told you so...but!

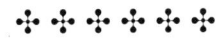

✣ ✣ ✣ ✣ ✣ ✣

The war was over. The Officers' Mess sent a truck some miles to get some special wine to celebrate the King's birthday and I happened to bump into one of the Mess Stewards. He was a lovely old cockney - in peace times an Express Milkman - and for some reason I was his mentor. He came to me with all his troubles and concerns and on this occasion he came up to me very long in the mouth. "I'm fed up with those bleedin' Officers, Tommy", said the steward. "What's up Bill?", I enquired. "Well", continued the hapless soul, "they reckon I've mucked-up the wine. They told me to de-something-or-other the wine." "Decant it?", I suggested. "Yeah, that's it....so anyway, I diluted the stuff and they're not very happy at all..."

✢ ✢ ✢ ✢ ✢ ✢

M G D'Arcy Esq - Devon

A CONUNDRUM OF WIT AND REPARTEE

I'm no rifle-range-warrior, assault-course-expert, kill-at-50-yards-with-my-bare-hands-commando – not me sir, but together with the troopers of Skinner's Horse; the RFs from Hounslow; the Cameroonians; the Punjabis and the Mahrattas, my pals and I, (the 17 rounds-a-minute wallahs called 'Gunners'), still have a tale or two to tell! How can we - unknown and unglorified – possibly have stories to match the 'heroes' of the Guards, Commandos and Paras? And with the Light Infantry marching at 160 to the minute, surely they cover more ground than the rest of us, don't they? But with the Mountain Artillery out-marching anyone on two or four legs, I think we experts know better and I think my father who marched with them to Llasa in Tibet in 1904 knew very well too......I bet he had a few funny tales to tell!

✢ ✢ ✢ ✢ ✢ ✢

As for us at the Omars, we always had a laugh about the time a Jerry AP shot took the arm off one of the drivers – he was changing gear at the time.

While we were busy conjuring-up a new driver all he could

think about was how to get his wedding ring off his finger! But get it off he did – and quite easily too. By simply standing on the portion just above his elbow and pulling at the band of gold on the finger in question, it just slid off. He was clearly relieved and remarked quite casually, "She'd never forgive me if I lost the ***** thing!"

✣ ✣ ✣ ✣ ✣ ✣

There was the other time when we had to leave a position in a bit of a hurry – in fact we left in a bit of a blasted rush and I had to travel for about 4 miles on the step of a limber. When we came to a halt I was told in no uncertain terms by a Number 1 (not ours), that it was dangerous to travel in such a way. Bearing in mind the state of the position we had just left, it was not the first time I had cause to doubt the army's mentality and the genetic legitimacy of some Numbers 1!

✣ ✣ ✣ ✣ ✣ ✣

Another time - out of contact with the enemy – we were showing some Young Officers the effects of air-burst and fragmentation. After firing twenty rounds in the general direction of a galvanised mock-up, we took the would-be officers along to inspect the damage for themselves.

Approaching the cluster of buildings, what should we see emerging from the rubble but a very unkempt and extremely irate chap. It transpired that he was a tramp who used the tumble-down hut as his home whenever he was in the area. No longer such a good idea it seemed!

✣ ✣ ✣ ✣ ✣ ✣

During the same practice, I'll never forget the sergeant major in charge demonstrating how to destroy excess charges – 50 bags of the stuff. He lined them all up, broke one open and lit the lot – one problem – he was standing down wind! Those damned YOs chortled most unkindly as 'the one who knows' eventually emerged from the scene with the shortest back-and-sides...and eyebrows ever seen!

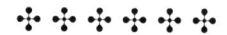

✥ ✥ ✥ ✥ ✥ ✥

Then it was back to Woolwich having been torpedoed en route to Liverpool. We arrived at 2am, all we had was what we stood-up in. Our kit, including my hat - was now in the hands of one Davy Jones. After our mammoth trip I ventured to ask the BSM – all British Warm and shiny ball buttons – for a cup of tea. "Sorry lad", came the reply, "don't you know there's a war on?" We were shown our bed space for the night, it was the guardroom floor. "Sorry about this" said the BSM, "there's a war on you know." Come the morning, the BSM – most definitely unblooded by action – asks about the whereabouts of my kit – nothing about how I travelled to Woolwich or from where. "Sorry BSM, the only person who knows the answer to that question is Davy Jones." "And 'oo might Davy Jones be then lad?" I felt like giving-up! "You want to look after your kit lad", continued Einstein, "there's people out there risking their lives on those convoys bringing kit like yours over 'ere. There's a war on you know and those German submarines don't give you a second chance!"

✥ ✥ ✥ ✥ ✥ ✥

Meanwhile back at the sharp end of things, there was the dumbo on sentry-go who gave the RSM a butt salute when said Brother of Allah visited the Guard Room..you don't make that mistake twice! We heard the irate WO's elephant trumpet roar from where we were in the Gun Park.. but there was worse to come! When the poor unfortunate was asked by the slightly cooled-off RSM if he had ever seen these before (pointing to the Royal Arms on his sleeve), he replied; "Yes Sir, on a cocoa tin..."

✢ ✢ ✢ ✢ ✢ ✢

Then there was the day our MO had cause to inspect one of the lads with a fluid-filled scrotum – huge it was! The MO was a wonderful chap and suggested he'd indent for a wheelbarrow in which our friend could transport his encumbrance.....

✢ ✢ ✢ ✢ ✢ ✢

And there's many more, but this one's your last! We were going back to camp having caught the last train. The carriage was a no-corridor type and six of us were lolling half a sleep having imbibed too much of the local brew. The train was chugging along as the old steam locals were wont when all of a sudden the door swings open and in walks a Canadian paratrooper, cigarette between his lips and saying, "Any of you guys got a light?" Having got one, out the door he went – presumably back the way he'd come and not one of us batted an eye! I can't imagine what an over sensitive Number 1 might have said about such a dangerous carry-on!

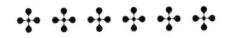

✢ ✢ ✢ ✢ ✢ ✢

R Duck Esq - London.

VERY REGIMENTAL

There's a Regimental March Past
And a Regimental do.
Get a Regimental haircut
The Regiment's expecting you.
Wear your Regimental cuff-links
And your Regimental tie
And when you march past
Look your Regimental Colonel in the eye.
There's a Regimental party
In the Regimental bar.
And your Regimental comrades
Will come from near and far.
The Regimental booze-up
Will end-up in the Regimental mist
But damned if I'll attend another do
To get Regimentally p*****d!

✢ ✢ ✢ ✢ ✢ ✢

F R E Durie Esq - Argyll.

RULES IS RULES

In 1941 I was a Troop Commander in a Light Anti Aircraft Regiment recently moved from Dover to Essex. Shortly before my appointment, I was told the following account of an incident which had affected a similar regiment after its own relocation from the South Coast to Cambridgeshire.

In regiments such as ours, the Gun Position was a defended area encircled by singly sited bofors usually commanded by a sergeant and security of the position was – as might be expected – of particular concern.

An Anti Aircraft Command Order of the day enforced the ruling that no strangers were permitted onto Gun Positions unless accompanied by an officer of the respective battery. The extent to which this ruling was enforced varied. In the Dover area security was taken very seriously but away from the coast it was perhaps slightly slacker.

The regiment in question had taken the position over in the morning and understandably was not entirely au fait with the intricacies of its new area of responsibility. That afternoon, a staff car driven by a brigadier drew-up at one of the sites. Leaving his car, he approached the sentry and introduced himself as the regiment's new Brigade Commander. Like most unexpected visits by senior officers, his intention was to inspect the site. Unlike many such sorties however, the brigadier did not bargain on what lay ahead!

Rather taken-aback at the arrival of a brigadier, the sentry called the sergeant to his post and explained the officer's presence to him. Sensing he may well be being tested on his knowledge and adherance to security rulings, the sergeant followed his own orders to the letter and informed the brigadier that he was not to be permitted onto the position without an accompanying Battery Officer.

Not happy at the news, the visitor became increasingly aggravated, but refusing to buckle under continued pressure, the NCO remained true to his instructions until – obviously at the end of his tether – the officer took the law into his own hands. Blustering forward, re-writing Army Standing Orders in his wake, the brigadier attempted to force his way past the sentry. But the steadfast sergeant was having none of it. Waving goodbye to what could well have been a promising army career, he called-up two gunners and – gesticulating wildly - ordered them to lock the supposed brigadier in the Guard Room.

With the said officer adding disturbing sound-effects to what was without doubt a fairly tense situation, the sergeant decided it was time to follow perhaps the greatest army tradition of all time. Telephoning his Troop Commander, he managed rather nicely to step under the all-important umbrella, thereby deflecting – albeit partially – any flak which may well come his way.

Taking a far less subtle side-step out of the crisis, the Troop Commander opted simply to pass the buck to the Adjutant and not surprisingly on hearing about the hub-bub, the Adjutant contacted the Brigade Major at Brigade HQ. If nothing else, the brigadier's visit was testing admirably the chain of command within the newly encumbered regiment!

In no time, it was confirmed that the Brigade Commander was indeed out on one of his snap inspections of gun-sites under his command. Things were looking a trifle sticky and, with the disturbing image of a red-faced brigadier behind bars bearing down on them, a rather top-heavy cortege soon drew-up at the respective gun-site.

This was perhaps not the best of starts for a newly-arrived regiment and as might be expected, everyone and his dog turned-up to view the damage: the Brigade Major, the CO, his Adjutant, the BC and the Troop Commander were ready for anything.

On the positive identification and subsequent release of the brigadier, all hell let loose. Placing the sergeant and two gunners concerned under close arrest, the former captive stormed-off leaving an understandably distressed CO pining once again for the chalky gun-sites of Dover.

Seeking advice or perhaps a shoulder to cry on, the Commanding Officer contacted the G1 at Divisional Headquarters and poured-out his woes to what he hoped would be a sympathetic ear. But it wasn't until well into the narrative that he realised he was in fact talking directly to the general himself. As the situation unveiled further, the general said he would be at RHQ in an hour and in due course an even larger cortege drew-up at the gun-site.

In front of his G1, the brigadier and his Brigade Major, the CO and his Adjutant and all the battery officers, the general asked for the three prisoners to be brought before him. On their arrival, he unleashed a barrage of praise onto the sergeant for his unstinting obeyance of the security ruling and to a stunned audience, ordered the brigadier to release them all from close arrest.

The brigadier departed on 'sick leave' that night and was shortly 'boarded' out of the army on 'medical grounds'. He was an old man and perhaps deserved a less humble departure for he chose the let-out he was offered rather than face a Court of Inquiry which could well have led him to a court martial.

✢ ✢ ✢ ✢ ✢ ✢

V Ellender Esq – Kessingland

TUNNEL TALES OF DOVER

During Christmas 1939 I was based at Dover Castle - well-known for the many tunnels and caves built within its walls. On one occasion shortly before I left for France, an ATS girlfriend and I found ourselves with the rare opportunity of spending a romantic time alone inside one of the tunnels. Sad to say though, after a few minutes all the lights went out leaving the place in complete darkness. We had turned a few corners since arriving in the tunnel and for the life of me I couldn't remember how to get out! Our predicament served to stifle any chance of romance and after a few moments of panic, my companion broke into an uncontrollable bout of screaming. Eventually her cries for help were answered by a passing ARP Warden who led us out to safety, no doubt wondering what we doing down in the tunnels in the first place! So much for romance – I never did see Eve again.

✥ ✥ ✥ ✥ ✥ ✥ ✥

The tunnels certainly were an important part of life at the castle though. I remember late on Christmas Eve I was in my billet with a few other lads when our Sergeant came into the room in search of two volunteers. It seemed that the light bulbs illuminating one of the tunnels had developed a rather uncanny habit of disappearing under the coats of soldiers and airmen as they passed through it. With another gunner, I was detailed to go down to the tunnel to act as an overt deterrent to any would-be bulb thief.

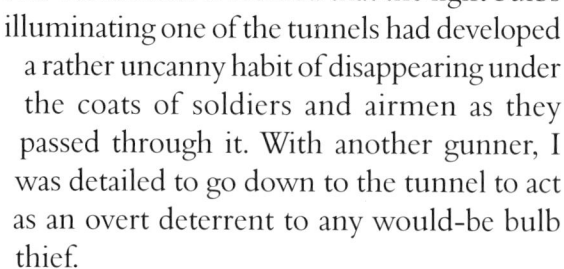

A short while after, we heard the sound of approaching footsteps and taking refuge in the recess of a nearby unlit tunnel, prepared to react to any untoward activity. As the chaps reached us - they were from the RAF - one of their number got caught short! He then proceeded to relieve himself only inches from where we were hiding.

There's only a certain amount that a man can put-up with in the course of his duty and as far as I was concerned, being used as a public convenience wasn't included. The last thing the hapless airman expected as he enjoyed the very personal pleasure of releasing the pressure in his bladder was a voice from nowhere stating very shortly and sharply, "WATCH IT!". Clearly shocked, the airman and his colleagues tore out of the tunnel leaving the two of us in hysterics - fit to bust! For some reason, the 'talk of the camp' next day was of an unknown headless drummer seen marching down the tunnel!

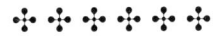

✤ ✤ ✤ ✤ ✤ ✤

General Sir Martin Farndale KCB
Master Gunner St James' Park

KEEPING UP APPEARANCES

Some years ago I was appointed as Honorary Colonel of a Yorkshire Territorial regiment and they decided to dine-me-in one day in January 1980 in one of their drill halls which did not have a kitchen. On such occasions, the food was provided by a contracted company which cooked the meals in its own kitchens and then transported the finished product by road to the drill hall.

On the day of my visit, it was snowing very heavily and by the time I arrived with the Commanding Officer to inspect the Guard of Honour, it was snowing heavier than ever. The Second in Command - who was also responsible for organising the evening - greeted us and told us that due to the weather, he had moved the guard inside. I went inside to meet a splendid guard but inevitably we were all a bit close to each other!

While I received the guard I overheard that which I was not meant to hear. It was the Second in Command saying to the CO in loud whisper, "Colonel, we have a problem, the vehicle bringing the dinner is upside down in a ditch about ten miles away and we have no dinner. I've laid on a Beating of Retreat to keep him happy while I sort it out."

I tried to act as if I was oblivious to anything being wrong and complemented the CO for not telling me about the beating retreat which was a great favourite and came as a nice surprise. About half an hour later it was announced that a dinner was ready but it was slightly different!

We formally went into a splendid dining room with the band playing 'The Roast Beef of Old England' and then after a solemn grace thanking the good Lord for that which we were about to receive – (the Colonel told me he was desperate by this time) – we were each issued with a plate of Chinese Take Away!

The dinner became a wonderful occasion and bound me to my new regiment in a very special way; you can guess how I was dined out eight years later!

✢ ✢ ✢ ✢ ✢ ✢

W Francis Esq - Leeds

SHEEP-SHANKED

As one of the Hoare-Belisha 'boys' required to join the forces prior to the start of World War Two, I was posted to 7th Medium Regiment RA and immediately became part of the original Army of The Nile – subsequently the 8th Army.

In June 1940, The Battle Axe Company was ordered into the desert for the first time. After an initial advance, we then withdrew until January 1941, when we advanced again to just outside Derna. It was when we were out of action, waiting I think for a replacement gun barrel, that in the distance I saw what looked like a herdsman tending his flock of sheep. Fresh meat was scarce at the time and the thought of adding to our diet a few morsels of succulent lamb proved too much of an opportunity to miss.

Calling to my mate, I told him my ruse and suggested he accompany me to the vicinity of the grazing herd – with his rifle. My plan was simple. Jim would 'persuade' the Arab that one sheep wouldn't be too much to spare. Such a timely diversion would enable me to grab one of the beasts, wrestle it to the cookhouse – *et voila* – fresh meat for one and all!

Jim agreed and with the Arab suitably threatened, I grappled with the largest sheep of the flock. With the beast on my back – and it was far heavier than I imagined a sheep could be, I staggered back towards the lines and eventually dumped the smelly and clearly distressed sheep next to the cookhouse.

Hanging onto the animal in case it escaped, I waited for the arrival of the cook to establish what culinary surprise he would conjure-up from our trophy. He eventually arrived and rather than congratulate us on our sheep-napping skills, he stared at us in obvious dismay. "What the hell have you got there then?", enquired the cook. "A big fat sheep", I replied. "You stupid sod! That's not a sheep, that's a goat - and a pregnant one at that..." Well, how was I to know? - how was a stupid cockney kid who had never seen a sheep before in his life know the difference. Simple wasn't I ?

✠ ✠ ✠ ✠ ✠ ✠

MALEME MELEE

Later on that year, the Battery found itself in Greece and after an argument with a Stuka dive-bomber, I became ensconced inside an Australian field hospital where I awaited evacuation to Crete. Once there, and having been given the all-clear to return to duties, I was posted to the RHQ of a New Zealand Infantry Battalion headed by a lieutenant. At the time, the German paras were beginning to land in force at Maleme aerodrome and the officer decided it would be a good defensive move to lay some mines to slow the German advance. As he carried-out his plan, a party of us attempted to drown the noise of his digging by firing a few shots in the general direction of the enemy. The process of laying the mines was a very noisy business and it was difficult to differentiate the sound of our rifles above the sound of the digging.

Things were going according to plan until the 'Kiwi' at the head of the party became increasingly aggravated: "Hey, who the hell's throwing stones." He clearly hadn't grasped what was going on – and just as well – when we got back to our dug-outs, there was a worryingly large dent in his steel helmet, I wonder how that got there!

✤ ✤ ✤ ✤ ✤ ✤

TIME SPENT ON RECCE...

It was March 1945 and the Battery was at Appledoorn. The HQ was sited a good distance from the designated sleeping quarters and one night, an officer who had not had time to recce the lay of the land lost sight of his guide as they followed a narrow path – via a farmyard – to the resting area. During his momentary loss of contact with the guide, the officer somehow managed to find the farm's cesspit and it was only after his cries had been heard by the Signals Sergeant that he was rescued.

The incident, although highly regrettable did, nonetheless, lend an air of gravity to proceedings and Gunners from near and far went out of their way to catch a glimpse of the cesspit. A brigadier from HQ was so interested, he made a number of sorties to the site – three in all – and on each occasion had to be revived from the hilarity by a good snort of the finest champagne. Perhaps the only other officer – apart from he who fell-in – who failed to see the funny side immediately, was the junior officer who had been the guide for his hapless senior....he went into hiding for a number of days!

Reverend G W Glew(Hon CF)
Canterbury Branch RAA

BETTER THE DEVIL YOU KNOW

During the Normandy Landings, I was a signaller with a 5.5 Regiment attached to 3 Infantry Brigade. Together with a mixture of our Guns, Matador Limbers, (a few) tanks, 3 Tonners and radio trucks, we embarked aboard a landing ship at Gosport en route to Sword Beach on the French coast. About half a mile from our landing site, the Guns and their towers were transferred onto a Rhino and, seizing the chance of a 'dry landing', I joined with a few other signallers on top of the steel boxes from which the Rhino was made.

As we chugged towards the beach at about 3 knots (I think it was top speed), we noticed that to our front and left an alarming number of extremely large splashes were appearing in the water with increasing regularity. It didn't take us long to realise that we were being ranged by a gun battery further inshore which had obviously not been softened-up by the earlier bombardments. The splashes got nearer and those of us aboard the Rhino became rather tense.

Amid our increasing concern, a rather profound comment ensued from the lips of one of our number; "If they get any nearer, I'm going to swim for it!" "I wouldn't do that if I were you", came a response from another who was half lying down and looking into the sea; "there's an 'ell of a lot of jelly fish down there....and they don't 'alf sting."

Despite the incoming shells and despite the uncertainty of what lay ahead, the severity of our predicament was forgotten. Shortly after this period of hilarity, HMS Warspite engaged the troublesome enemy battery with a salvo from her guns and fortunately for us, silenced that particular source of danger.

✤ ✤ ✤ ✤ ✤ ✤

CHAR BURN

Some weeks after the landings, I spent a few days at the Gun Position (a rest from the OP end). One afternoon all was quiet and we were called to collect our tea meal; a brew from a dixie of compo tea, a pack of hardtack biscuits and – to share between two men – a tin of sardines in cottonseed oil.

As we filed-off in pairs and returned back to our slit trenches laden down with our veritable feast, a battery of 88s' opened-up from somewhere in the distance and it wasn't long before rounds started landing on our position. Understandably, our pace increased and we dived to find cover in the nearest available slit trench. I was the second one to find shelter in a partly submerged trench and almost immediately, I felt the weight of others as they too avoided the incoming shells. Before long, the trench became full - so much so that the last man in must surely have been above ground level.

The bombardment continued and one round in particular landed very close to our position (we later learned that it had set fire to the cam net of the gun next to us). As it hit the ground, I felt a red hot pain in my neck. "I've been hit!", I yelled in the best voice I could manage. "Sorry old chap," said a very refined voice above me, "I'm afraid I slopped some of my tea when that one went off, it won't happen again." (Only an assistant Command Post Officer could have done and said a thing like that!).

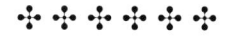

✣ ✣ ✣ ✣ ✣

Colonel G S Hatch CBE – Woolwich

THE SPEECHLESS MAJOR

Despite fresh memories of their sufferings elsewhere, by early 1948, sympathy for the Jewish cause had waned a little amongst many in the British Forces stationed in Palestine. This estrangement was attributable largely to the excessive zeal displayed from time to time by certain elements of the swelling Jewish population in furthering their attempts to acquire, before the impending British departure, arms which were the property of His Majesty's Government.

Various clandestine and semi-clandestine armed groups had developed some singularly unattractive habits. One of these is exemplified by the events described in the account below which deals with a raid upon a camp and its armouries.

I was by this time a member of a detached battery ('U' Bty) of 12th Anti-Tank Regiment. The Battery task in these closing weeks of the mandate was to supply a mobile presence along the westerly section of the road linking Jaffa with Jerusalem. The aim was to inhibit as far as possible, certain obstreperous activities on the part of local Arab patriots.

These somewhat haphazardly organised warriors were intent upon interrupting the passage of Jewish lorry-convoys which carried goods and warlike stores to the Jewish population in the Eternal City - Jerusalem. In those somewhat hectic sunny Spring days, all kinds of groups were forming themselves into military or para-military organisations or cadres; and there was, to say the least, a distinctly tense atmosphere.

It had become, however, increasingly difficult for our Battery in particular, to take part enthusiastically and with its usual panache, in hazardous operations designed to separate the contestants along the road. This was a direct consequence of one aspect of an action involving the other three batteries of the regiment.

On the occasion in question a large raiding party from a highly effective Jewish irregular force called the Irgun Zvai Leumi, then operating under the direction of a later Prime Minister (Mr Begin), had driven up to the regiment's main camp very early one morning attired in British uniforms and driving what appeared to be British vehicles. They had by this simple ruse forced an entry into the camp and the ploy had gained them sufficient time and surprise to shoot, from the leading vehicle, the sentry on duty at the barrier and also the covering sentry in a sandbagged emplacement further back. There followed a 'Help-Yourself' visit to two battery armouries. The Commanding Officer, Lt-Colonel Hildebrand, was killed while gallantly attempting to rush an armoured vehicle and attack its occupants. And before leaving, the detachment which had throughout these events held the remaining members of the by-now disarmed guard at gun point shot their captives dead.

With this immediate memory, it became increasingly difficult to persuade British soldiers to deter Arab irregulars from attacking Jewish convoys as they ran the gauntlet through the hills on their journey to Jerusalem. However, there always seems to be someone who fails to receive current news. In this instance, it was a distinctly portly major in the Royal Army Pay Corps. His intervention in one engagement shortly after the raid described above was a memorable event which I witnessed at close quarters.

Early one crisp, clear morning (they were all clear, crisp mornings) in the foothills near a place called Bab el Wad, where stood a shot-up and consequently disused one-pump petrol station, near a junction north of Hebron (I saw this place again quite recently, now adorned by a modern, brightly painted Shell filling station), we came upon what appeared to be a convoy ambush in noisy progress.

On such occasions it was not always easy to pinpoint the marksmen on the hillsides amongst the rock-strewn scrub. Our customary procedure for dealing with such situations was therefore to encourage the assailants to depart by lobbing a few 2-inch mortar bombs in their direction. This invariably cleared the neighbourhood and restored the desired state of Pax Artillery.

On this occasion, however, an unusual sight greeted our gaze as we rounded a bend near the sound of firing. We could see at the junction a lone 15cwt vehicle. Standing-up in the cab, his head and shoulders protruding through the hole which was provided for the purpose was the aforementioned portly Major. I can see him now: he looked very much like Ronnie Barker. He was by himself and dressed in Service Dress and Sam Browne belt, with his peaked cap firmly in place. On what mission he was bent I cannot say. He was blazing away with his Bren gun, firing magazine after magazine, spraying the hillsides with great abandon. I remember feeling a little apprehensive lest one of his more grandiose sweeps should take in our vehicles too.

Just beside me was a certain Gunner Heap manning a Bren gun. He was a bespectacled soldier whose name perfectly described his everyday appearance. Although somewhat trigger-happy by nature, in default of any semblance of a target, even Gunner Heap was not at that moment engaged in his customary practice of applying prophylactic fire, either accidentally or through over-keenness in anticipation of orders. Surveying open-mouthed the scene of action, he muttered incredulously, 'Christ Almighty...it's the Galloping Major himself!!'

Just then there was a lull in the general exchange of unaimed fire ahead of us. Presumably having exhausted his supply of ammunition, the intrepid major sat down abruptly and without saying a single word (perhaps he did not speak to Subalterns before lunch) drove briskly off in the direction of Jerusalem, no doubt to put himself in for an MC!

I never identified the Speechless Major, nor can I say how many other single-handed battles like the one we encountered at what I now call Pay Corps Corner he entered. If the brave major ever reads these words, I hope that he may reload his old computer, reach for a brandy and rest content, for I can confidently assure him that the finest traditions of his Corps would in similar circumstances still be upheld today by any Paymaster. This includes our own here at Woolwich, even though she is only 5ft 2ins in height and she would therefore, in order to become a Brave Defender in the mould of the Speechless Major of 1948, without doubt have to stand on the seat!

Reproduced by kind permission of Gunner magazine.

✤ ✤ ✤ ✤ ✤

Lieutenant-Colonel H W Hawkins TD - Liverpool.

GUNNER STEW

On an Anti-Aircraft Gun site in the early part of the last war, the Section-Commander was informed that a General Officer would be inspecting his position that very afternoon. There was insufficient time to make proper preparations and to carry-out the usual 'bull' which accompanied such inspections, so the Section-Commander made a quick appreciation of the situation. He knew very well that few Generals had any knowledge of modern anti-aircraft gunnery and Radar and so would avoid inspecting the Gun Park. This being the case, he decided to concentrate on the cleanliness of both the cookhouse and the latrines.

Calling his Battery Cook, he explained that the General would be inspecting the cookhouse and so the highest standards would be expected. Before dismissing him, he told him to put on a clean pair of overalls and to have a basin of soapy water nearby to keep his hands clean at all times.

The inspection went well until they came to the cookhouse.

On seeing the 'Stock-Pot' which usually delighted Generals, he plunged his cane into its contents to give it a good stir. Suddenly the General's face dropped. His cane had caught on something at the bottom of the pot and worse still, it had actually got stuck! The cane was indeed securely cemented in the pot, but like all good fishermen, the General persevered. Watched with fatal fascination by all the escorting officers, he gradually brought his cane to the surface and there, stuck at the end of it were the cook's dirty overalls!

✤✤ ✤ ✤ ✤ ✤

P Head Esq - Richmond
MALTESE CLAP TRAP

In early 1953 while serving with 49th Field Regiment in Cyprus, I was ordered home to attend the War Office Selection Board and was given a rare place on a flight to the UK. For some reason – which was never made clear – I was ordered off the plane at Malta and told to wait for later transport.

Feeling like some form of Gunner gypsy, I was billeted with a Heavy Anti Aircraft regiment at Imtarfa and assigned to a troop to earn my keep while in transit - Gunner nature abhors a vacuum.

The day came for BC's Orders - one of the Gunners had a misdemeanour needing suitable attention and being the only Troop Officer in sight, I had to attend. I knew him not – nor he me, but due form had to be done and seen to be done. Outside the BC's office the usual loud voices could be heard.

"Cap off!.. belt off!.. ri-iight turn! qu-iiick march..deft-dight-deft-dight!" In through the swung-open door came the stamping procession of the escort, the defendant and the order-barking BSM. "H-aaalt!..ri-iight turn!." "24675010 Gunner Smith – SIR!"

With due gravity, the BC read out the charge: "24675010

Gunner Smith, you are charged under Section 40 of the Army Act: Conduct to the prejudice of good order and military discipline, in that you on such-and-such-a-night did render yourself unfit for military duty in that you did negligently contract a venereal disease. Do you plead guilty or not guilty?"

"Guilty, Sir".

"Very well Smith, will you take my award, or do you wish to appear before the Commanding Officer?"

"I'll take your award Sir."

"Very good Smith, seven days confined to barracks".

The mood in the office changed noticeably. The BC removed his cap and turned positively avuncular.

"Now then Smith, you have obviously been very er - silly.. but we do of course need to find out where you managed to pick the-um - the-er wretched stuff up from. The health people will have to check it all out. Understood?"

Shuffling his feet, a hangdog expression descended over Smith's face.

"Speak-up lad..", muttered the BSM, "..the Major asked you a question."

"W-well Sir", stammered a crimsoning Smith, "..it was in the Street of the Immaculate Conception..."

The BC's Orders simply collapsed!

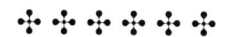

✥ ✥ ✥ ✥ ✥ ✥

FOWL PLAY

During the Malay Emergency, I was privileged to command a separate troop of Malay Gunners from 1st Singapore Regiment. There was a small handful of British ranks – one of whom was a signaller and in civilian life, a poacher. He was without doubt an asset to the Command Post and had ingenious ways of supplementing our diet. By draping a net under the front axle of the Command vehicle, for example, any stray chickens strolling through a village as we sped through it would simply be scooped-up and hey presto – SUPPER!

On one occasion we staged overnight in a Police compound. This not only gave us local security, but also a chance to get ourselves organised until the next deployment at first light. The compound housed the police constables and their families, and as we bustled about our business I noticed in the corner, a bunch of women clucking around. My mind was certainly elsewhere at the time and I thought little more of the incident until later that evening while dining with my Gun Position Officer at the home of the Sikh Police Inspector.

As we started to tuck into the delicious curry, our host broached what must have been a very difficult matter. He explained - rather awkwardly - that a duck had gone absent without leave at about the time our Guns had arrived in the compound. The local womenfolk had scoured the place for the thing and were now most annoyed at the thought of the duck being served on someone else's plate! The curry turned to ashes. That confounded signaller, how could he do such a thing on our own door step...and in a police compound for Heaven's sake?

At the earliest opportunity, we excused ourselves and roared back to the lines and roused the slumbering signaller. After a period of intense questioning, he managed to convince us that as a poacher, he knew far better than to plan such a ruse - especially at a place crawling with so many police. But the blasted thing had to be somewhere. We searched every vehicle, tent, box and crate that night but nothing - not a bone nor a feather nor a fowl in any form whatsoever could be found.

Making an early call to the Duty Officer to thank him for his help etc, we left at first light and were still none the wiser as to the whereabouts of the duck – dead or alive.

In due course we arrived at the day's first gun position. The targets we were to engage had been plotted and the fire orders were issued.

"Number 1! – one round gunfire".

No response, but from my position in the Command Post I could see some considerable scurrying around Number 1 sub-section.

"Number 1! – one round gunfire"

Still no response. I ran over to the Malay Bombardier who was investigating the delay.

"Can't fire Tuan!", says he.

"Why not?", says I incensed that my fire plan was going down the tube in front of my eyes.

Slamming open the breech, the reason became crystal clear. Out popped a perfectly formed, if somewhat oily duck – as dead as they come. It tasted delicious!

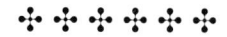

✠ ✠ ✠ ✠ ✠ ✠

FAYRE EXCHANGE?

Without doubt, exercises in north Germany during the mid-1950s really spoiled a lad's social life! They were made even more burdensome when they took place in the Hohne Ranges where, as a Light Anti Aircraft Regiment, we were not permitted to fire and had to pretend to be combative while the Field Gunners and tanks charged around the place playing for real.

Our guns were dispersed around the exercise area to give local air defence and each gun position was self-contained and self sufficient with its own rations. We were issued with the usual dull and uninspiring compo rations but for some reason, the particularly foul tins of fish met the German palate and so the enterprising could usually barter with locals living nearby for eggs to add a bit of luxury to mealtimes. On one occasion, the local farmer on whose land we had deployed became openly displeased with the presence of so many Tommies on his patch. He was having none of it – it seemed the chance of a quick barter here and there was definitely out of the question.

On my rounds of the position, it was obvious the boys were tucking into something a little more than standard-issue compo. Very much aware of the ill-feeling prevailing between us and the locals, I enquired discreetly about the provenance of the lavish fresh vegetables.

"Don't worry Sir", came the reply. "We went into the potato field after dark, and took some out of the ground."

"But that's stealing", I protested - fearing a local uprising.

"Oh no Sir, we buried a tin of dried potato in its place!".

✥ ✥ ✥ ✥ ✥ ✥

S Hutson Esq – Lincoln

CHINDIT CHALLENGE

On leaving the desert in 1942, 60th Field Regiment transferred from the 7th Armoured Division (Desert Rats) to the 70th British Infantry Division (later to become the 3rd Indian Division) and was almost immediately grabbed by General Orde Wingate to become part of his second 'Chindit' Expedition.

The regiment handed-over its 25-pounders and concentrated on its infantry drills. Despite this change in role however, it did retain its Gunner identity and became 60 Column RA and 88 Column RA as part of 23 Brigade.

Soon after deployment, the unit was infiltrating through the Naga Hills and Manipur to get around the back of General Saito's 31st Division of crack Japanese troops. Both columns were in a bad way. Malaria and dysentery were rife and many of the gunners were suffering from jungle sores and lack of food. Despite this rather disheartening situation though, General Saito's predicament was considerably worse. There had been some intense fighting and it was clear he was never going to take Kohima. 23 Brigade had almost completely cut-off his food and ammunition supply and to compound the issue, the Brigade was also blocking his escape route.

Both Gunner columns were involved in small-scale ambushes and on this occasion we were operating together - two platoons from 60 Column and one from 88 Column. We were told by a tea or rubber planter that his staff had seen upto 1000 'Japani' on top of the next hill. Some were very ill with 'beri-beri' and the remainder were not in very good health at all. We were well-versed in the art of surprise and more than able to cause a high degree of mayhem in a very short space of time but we did of course have to ensure that the enemy were not given sufficient time to realise our limited number!

It was decided to launch an attack using 14 and 15 Platoons from 60 Column - each climbing opposite sides of the very steep hill. The officer in charge of the assault carried a Very pistol to be fired when it was light enough for us to see and dark enough to add confusion to the sleeping enemy.

We climbed through the Stygian darkness, and moved silently through the undergrowth to a position within striking distance of the Japs. Dawn broke and when the officer considered it light enough, he fired a red Very light.

14 platoon rose as one and with Sten guns blazing, we went straight into the attack. From the other side of the hill top, silence reigned....but the 20 of us charging towards the enemy were oblivious to our solitude - and probably just as well.

The minutes ticked by, and there was still no sign that 15 Platoon were planning to join-in with the proceedings. We continued with the assault - spraying death and destruction in our path, but as usual, the Japanese were quick to react. Within 5 minutes they were returning fire and so in view of our size, a quick withdrawal was signalled and executed with no losses to our own side.

Later that day we met-up with 15 Platoon and after a few choice words, the full story came-out. On the way-up to their position, they had got bogged-down in thick bamboo and creepers and had no means of informing the officer of their predicament. As a result, one of the Japs' crack-fighting-elite numbering 1000 had come under attack from 20 lightly-armed gunners and had suffered more than a bloody nose to boot. As nobody had been hurt, rather than causing a few heads to roll, the episode became a matter of immense amusement throughout the regiment!

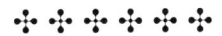

✤ ✤ ✤ ✤ ✤ ✤

J Ince Esq – Ontario, Canada
12 OCTU(HAC) RHA
Aldershot
January 1940

DOWN THE PAN

Drill Instructor Sergeant Muggeridge had a way with words! During his dealings with would-be officers on the Square at OCTU, his bon mots were memorable. This was one of his better displays.

The squad were not making much progress in developing their mastery of drill: Sergeant Muggeridge had seen enough. In exasperation and with a withering inflection in his voice, Muggeridge brought the scene before him to a halt. "GENTLEMEN..gentlemen...DO YOU know what your marching reminds me of?...S★★★!...YES S★★★! Your marching is nothing but S★★★!" He paused as he sought just the right words to convey the full force of his frustration. "That's it gentlemen.. bags of S★★★ that's what you are, bags of the stuff..and loosely packed at that!"

✣ ✣ ✣ ✣ ✣ ✣

61st Field Regiment
Neder Rijn, north of Njmegen
October 1944

FEATHERED FRENZY

The 61st Regiment was busy holding the advancing Allied left flank and for sometime had been subjected to some heavy and continuous attacks. It was also providing fire support to the troops of the 101st US Airborne Division who at that time were involved in some fairly intense hand-to-hand combat.

Understandably, the importance of artillery support at this time was vital, if nothing more, it was extremely good for the morale of the troops who benefited enormously from the application of accurate and timely shelling to their front.

Meanwhile at the Gun-end, the 10 mile long supply corridor through which the ammunition passed, was experiencing problems of its own kind and hence ammunition resupply was becoming less reliable.

The young British officer responsible for calling fire ahead of the US advance was at one point told to relax his rate of fire as he had already expended the regiment's 24-hour allocation. Conditions being what they were, the captain managed to stymie such demands and after a few terse words, the shells continued to fall – much to the benefit of the US advance.

After a particularly vicious night, the troops found refuge in a nearby Dutch farm and to amuse themselves - or to relieve the stress of the night before – practiced their knife throwing skills on the chickens which roamed innocently outside the barn-turned-HQ.

Although grateful that the US troops had managed to dent further the withdrawing German army, the Dutch farmer was becoming slightly agitated that so many of his chickens were rapidly becoming no-more and his agitation strengthened when it became apparent that the troops present were obviously quick learners.

He made vain appeals to the American CO who, although sympathetic to his concerns, was met by comments from his men which implied that rather than getting demoralised about the fate of his livestock, the farmer should in fact be happy to be alive. The Dutchman finally turned to the British officer for support.

Having been through the turmoil of the night before, the captain understood the mood of the men, but perhaps his British up-bringing pricked his conscience and the lot of the farmer's rapidly diminishing feathered egg-producers was cause for concern. This Limey was indeed facing a tricky moment..a moment in which his discretion and morality would-be tested to the limit. How could a Limey make a stand for moral correctness before so many US paras? What exactly could he say which in some way would appeal to the softer side of these well-bloodied troops?

But fate had dealt him a powerful hand. He aired his concern for the chickens with the CO who then addressed his men. Essentially, the tenacity of the artilleryman was conveyed to the troops. The difficulties of ammunition supply were explained and the manner in which he had tersely demanded more artillery support for their advance the night before was brought to the fore. After the CO had said his piece, the wishes of the Limey were - with exception of the occasional muffled squawk and flurry of feathers met by the slumbering troops. Despite the ferocity of this particular theatre of war, the conscience of one artilleryman had thus been seen to evoke an element of Shakespearean tragedy: All's Well That End's Well - excepting of course from the view point of the feathered creatures with early walk-on parts!

✢ ✢ ✢ ✢ ✢ ✢

Major G Jacobs MBE RA(Retd) – Bickton
Trumpeter Jacobs
21 Heavy Battery
Mauritius
November 1937- April 1939

IF YOU CAN'T TAKE A JOKE...

Shortly after settling in at Vacoas Camp after six weeks at sea and only a mouth piece to keep my lips in trim, my fellow trumpeter asked if I would stand-in for him for the last three calls of the day; First and Last Post and Lights out. I was not very confident due to my lack of practice, but agreed.

Bringing my trumpet to my pursed lips, I sounded what I thought was First Post and to my astonishment in next to no time the Orderly Officer and Fire Picquet (complete with equipment) came running-up to me shouting "Where's the fire? Where's the fire!" Was it my poor sounding or a cunning ruse to embarrass the newly joined badgie?

TEMPUS FUGIT

One duty morning, I awoke 15 minutes late - PANIC! Still wearing my pyjamas, I dashed down to the parade ground and sounded 6am Reveille hoping nobody would have stirred sufficiently to report my tardy start to the day.

Feeling sure my crime had gone undetected and taking a final glance around me, I grabbed a nearby ladder and propped it up against the wall of the Battery Clock tower. Stepping deftly up the rungs, I managed to nudge the clock's hands to read 6am - certainly one way to make-up lost time!

But the danger of detection was still looming. Running swiftly-up the stairs and dressing hurriedly, I resumed my position on the parade ground and sounded the necessary call for 7am parade - 15 minutes late.

Not surprisingly, the BSM - Bertie Meyer - was soon at my side and quizzed me heatedly about my apparent late call. But pointing to the Battery Clock, I eventually managed to convince him that it was perhaps his time piece that was running a little ahead of time and not mine. Later that morning when the coast was clear, I hopped-up the ladder and put the clock onto the correct time. Tempus fugit!

Officer Cadet (Ex-WO1(SMAC)) G Jacobs
OCTU
nr Aldershot
April 1947

WHEN DRILL WASN'T ALL THAT BAD

When it came to rifle drill, I was - to put it mildly - indifferent. The periods left me quivering - especially when taken by the Guards CSM who took delight in intimidating anyone who didn't share his passion for the parade ground.

On one occasion we were formed-up ready for the period when 'The Voice' - RSM Brittan - appeared. To my horror he made straight for me and, opting for the more sinister approach to dealing with Potential Officers, he whispered in my ear the immortal line, "Fall out Cadet".

I was dumbstruck! What had I done? All kinds of thoughts went through my head as I was marched away, but more importantly, did whatever I had done merit a spell in the Guard Room?

Once clear of the square, I was halted and ordered to ground arms and stand easy for the next 45 minutes. Such an instruction was clear evidence that I was being given-up as a lost hope, or was I just so bad that I was ruining an otherwise passable squad? But I need not have worried. It seemed that RSM Brittan was reaching an important milestone in his own career. I was questioned nonstop by Brittan for the whole of the period about the pros and cons for a Regular WO1 taking a commission. The best drill period I ever had!

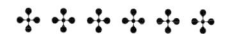

✣ ✣ ✣ ✣ ✣ ✣

M L James Esq BEM
Maritime Royal Artillery Old Comrades' Association
Sandown, Isle-of-Wight

NEARLY..BUT NOT QUITE

While serving in 114th(Sussex) Field Regiment at Eastbourne, one of our chaps - a coalman in Civvie Street - was promoted to Lance Bombardier. His first excursion with a file of men came shortly after promotion and during its passage around camp, the squad happened upon an officer on his rounds.

"Ey-es..Right", was followed by a very smart salute.

So far so good!

The officer returned the compliment and after an inordinate delay the long awaited response eventually came from the side of the file; "Ey-es.......back again!"

Oh dear.

✠ ✠ ✠ ✠ ✠ ✠

A Jenkins Esq - Portsmouth
53rd Worcestershire Yeomanry Regiment RA
33rd Parachute Light Regiment RA
7th Parachute Regiment RHA

MARRIED BLISS

I married my wife in 1949 and as was customary, was given leave to enjoy my first weeks of married life at home. We never knew where we would be going next so it was quite good for morale!

Towards the end of my matrimonial leave, I was dreading the thought of returning to work and would have done anything to stay at home a few days more. All too quickly though, my leave came to its end and I reluctantly packed my kit and caught the last train from Portsmouth to Salisbury to report for duty at the following morning's muster parade.

The journey was understandably quite miserable. The thought of leaving the wife back in Portsmouth was bad enough but as I had caught the evening's last train, I also faced the problem of getting from Salisbury station to our base at Bulford Camp as there would be no military transport to meet me. When the train pulled into the station, there was nothing I could do but resort to Shank's Pony and so, throwing my kit-bag over my shoulder I started the long trek from the station to camp - on foot.

I don't remember much about the journey. It was long and it was boring but in the early hours of the morning, I finally reached camp and fell into a deep sleep on the first unoccupied bed I could find. In fact, I fell asleep on a bed with no sheets and no mattress and collapsed - still wearing my overcoat - on some fairly uncomfortable army bed springs! The morning came fast and I was greeted back to army life by my sergeant looking fairly bemused.

Despite my efforts to prolong my leave to the last moment

and despite the ordeal of the previous night's mammoth trek from Salisbury station, somehow the army's communication network had gone seriously wrong. It seems the Battery Commander had decided to extend my leave for another week - but someone somewhere had forgotten to pass the message on!

✤ ✤ ✤ ✤ ✤ ✤

W J Meredith Esq - Swansea

TRENCH FOOT

It was April 1943 and 56 Heavy Regiment RA - as part of the 1st Army - was involved in the Medjez-El-Bab offensive in North Africa.

After a long day's disciplined convoy movement, the RHQ party were diverted off the road to establish a Command Post along the mountainside. It wasn't long before the RSM detailed the survey party to dig slit trenches and a mate and I were ordered to dig a trench immediately outside the Command Post.

As expected the ground was rock hard - quite possibly solid rock - and we were soon sweating our brows off in the heat. Come dusk, we had only managed to dig down about a foot and the ground seemed to be getting harder. To make matters worse, we spotted in the distance Major Arrowsmith - the Second-in-Command - and he was coming our way.

As the major approached our position, my mate leaned-over and whispered to me to get on my knees. By the time the officer could see us, we were apparently upto our necks in a trench and still beavering away with pick and shovel in hand. With his binoculars hanging around his neck, the major stood upright in his car and towering above us in the darkness enquired what we were both doing. "Digging a trench for you Sir", came our reply. "Do you think it's deep enough?"

"Of course it's deep enough! Do you think I'm afraid of the bloody Boche? Now get some sleep."

Still on our knees, we both saluted and automatically responded, "Very good, Sir". As the major's car drove on, we both did exactly as instructed - it wasn't everyday an order like that came your way!

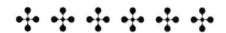

✣ ✣ ✣ ✣ ✣ ✣

Lieutenant-General Sir Dougals Packard - Lower Ufford, Suffolk

TOO CLOSE FOR COMFORT

During the Palestine rebellion shortly before the war, I commanded a troop stationed in Nablus Fort. One night, the Brigade Major from the Infantry Brigade rang through ordering us to fire on a certain range of hills from which the local Oozlebarts (rebels) were then firing. These hills had been registered from the fort by my predecessor and I gave out what I thought were the correct fire orders to engage the range of hills on the leftside of this valley.

We had fired a few rounds from our 3.7 howitzers mounted in the fort, when the Brigade Major rang through once again telling us that the enemy where moving further to the right. I ordered the guns to switch their fire a further 10 degrees to the right and after a few rounds, the telephone rang furiously once again.

"STOP!...STOP!.." - it was the Brigade Major. "STOP! - you are firing on this position. You must stop your guns - AT ONCE!".

The Brigade Major was not exaggerating. One of the rounds had fallen into the drawing room of one of the houses adjacent to his position. To make matters worse however, the damaged house was owned by non-other than the Mayor of Nablus. It transpired that my original orders to the guns had in fact brought fire down on the rightside of the valley and so when I ordered the switch to the right, the fire went much further than I intended.

The next day, I found myself on the mat before the brigadier. Fortunately, he accepted my excuse that the incident had happened in the heat of battle on a very wet night and that the register of targets had been drawn-up by someone else. It was indeed an unfortunate mistake and would not occur again.

The brigadier decided that the cost of the damage - £35.00 -

could be met by the State. His decision was passed to Divisional HQ in Haifa, whither I was duly ordered to report. Sadly, the Divisional Commander - later a celebrated Field Marshal in the desert - took a completely opposite view of the situation and ordered that unless I paid for the cost of the damage, he would report my name to the War Office. In those days, that was about a month's wages but as I had only recently earned my 'jacket' again, I did not wish my name to go anywhere near the War Office: I had no option but to pay. My wife never forgave the Field Marshal!

Later in my career when I was Chief of Staff to the Commander-in-Chief MELF, I had occasion to visit the Arab Legion in Jordan. My interviewer there was King Hussein's Chief-of-Staff who had previously been the Mayor of Nablus at the time I had been stationed at the fort. Needless to say, I did not mention the incident in his house!

✤ ✤ ✤ ✤ ✤ ✤

WJ Page Esq - Portsmouth.
Bombardier WJ Page
53rd Worcestershire Yeomanry Regiment RA
6th Airlanding Brigade

THE OLD 53rd

Where are those Gunners of the old 53rd?
Where have they gone?
Where did they go?
Remember the Horsa-Hammilcar
One gun, one trailer
One jeep,
six men too.
Remember the Ardennes'
Ice-cold snow
Where are the Gunners of the old 53rd?
Where have they gone?
Where have they goed?
Remember the Rhine
Its dusk smoke and rhyme.
Remember the gliders
That fell from the skies
Remember the comrades
That we left behind
Where are you Gunners of the old 53rd?

✥ ✥ ✥ ✥ ✥ ✥

HJ Porter Esq – Co Antrim

IF LOOKS COULD KILL

After the war, I commanded a TA Gunner Regiment in Northern Ireland which had seen service with the BEF and in South East Asia. Unlike the wartime regiment where all members were male, a number of ATS/WRAC operators had been enlisted to operate the Command Post - and they were splendid.

On his first visit to the regiment as Honorary Colonel, the former CO of the regiment was rather taken aback at seeing so many lovely girls in uniform for the first time. Unsure of how to deal with them, he was advised to simply chat to them individually and to ask a few pertinent questions in exactly the same way he would a male soldier.

The Colonel squared-up to a rather pretty girl and said, "Tell me dear, could you kill a man?" After a few seconds thought and much fluttering of her eyelashes, she replied, "Yes sir.....eventually!".

Her earnest response and superb timing quite literally brought the house down.

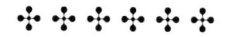

✤ ✤ ✤ ✤ ✤ ✤

Brigadier S P Robertson MBE TD JP DL - Orkney

NUN TOO PLEASED

After the cessation of hostilities in Italy, I heard a story which could well have been based on fact but was probably apocryphal... It occurred in a north Italian town with a large square at its centre which - when the availability of petrol permitted - the locals seemed to spend morning and evening roaring around on their motorcycles. On one side of the square the General had his HQ and on the other was a Nunnery headed by its Mother Superior.

There came a time when the Mother Superior could take no more of the annoying disturbances which prevailed whenever the petrol supplies became sufficiently abundant to allow the locals to partake of their noisy pastime. So bad was the noise that she asked the General if he could please do something about it. Not surprisingly he endeavoured to solve the problem in a most energetic way.

In his letter to the Mayor of the town it is reported that among other things, he complained bitterly "that the Mother Superior and he did not get a wink of sleep all night.....".

✣ ✣ ✣ ✣ ✣ ✣

RIGHT OF LINE

Another time - and this story is true - my Regiment was grounded on the banks of the Seine, our heavy transport having been taken away to do supply duties. We were bivouacked in a pine forest opposite Les Andleys and so far as I can remember the nearest town was called Louviers. We were out of action for two or three weeks and - taking a realistic view of the situation - the Medical Officer decided it would be a prudent step to inspect the local brothel.

Making another equally prudent step, he managed to cajole

his good friend the Quartermaster to accompany him on what could be a professionally hazardous house-call.

Arriving slightly before opening-time, the two waited patiently to undertake their cursory inspection of the premises. Shortly before the doors eventually opened, the two officers glanced over their shoulders and much to their consternation found themselves heading a queue of soldiers from various regiments awaiting the services therein...Needless to say they explained their presence to the waiting hordes...and I for one would have believed them!!!

✥ ✥ ✥ ✥ ✥ ✥

ALL BELT AND BRACES

Yet another true story is about my own Battery. After the war had ended we were quartered, in considerable comfort, in a distillery near Cologne. The new Brigadier had arrived from the UK to take command of the District and amongst other things had brought with him his pre-war ideas of discipline. In particular he was very strong on matters relating to dress and one morning my Battery Sergeant Major came to me with the latest order relating to how the men should wear their web braces.

BSM Salisbury was a splendid old regular Gunner and had been with me throughout the campaign. He was well-aware that my patience had been sorely tried by the continually evolving dress regulations and when I said that as far as I was concerned the men could wear their braces hanging around their bottoms he took it in the manner it was meant.

Next morning when I took Battery Parade, I was greeted by the BSM who - with a twinkle in his eye and perhaps just the hint of a grin - saluted smartly and reported "Battery ready for inspection as ordered - Sir."

It was a sight more worthy of a Bateman cartoon than a story, for everyone on parade had their webbing hanging down as I had decreed except me! (I might add that this display was a good example of the high morale which existed in the Battery and of the great understanding between all ranks - including the Battery Commander!)

✣ ✣ ✣ ✣ ✣ ✣

WEE ROBBIE'S DILEMMA

When I commanded the independent battery, 861 (Orkney and Zetland) Anti-Aircraft Battery RA TA, it won The Sunday Times Trophy - the then premier award for Anti-Aircraft Artillery. As a Battery, we were of course immensely proud of having achieved this, particularly as the field included many more anti aircraft regiments in comparison with today.

Such awards are usually presented in London's Guildhall, but in the late 1950s, 'Mohammet came to the Mountain', and the GOC Scotland, Lieutenant-General Sir George Collingwood, came to Orkney to present the Trophy. Before the event we entertained him at my house where my son Robbie - who was only about six or seven years old at the time - was introduced to the General. As they met, the General reached into the waistcoat pocket of his Mess Kit to give him half a crown and on finding nothing there, borrowed a coin from his ADC. As he offered the coin to my son who had witnessed the General's frantic search, Robbie in his innocence said: "Are you sure you can afford it, Sir?".

Future events cast their shadows before, and perhaps it is not surprising that he is now the Finance Manager of a sizeable international organisation!

✣ ✣ ✣ ✣ ✣ ✣

'ERSES' TO THE SPEY

This final memory, perhaps apocryphal, but quite likely true, was recounted to me by a Seaforth friend, and told by the late Major-General Ronnie Somerville - at that time the CRA - at the last Divisional Dinner of the Royal Artillery of the 51st Highland Division. It concerned a volunteer Battalion of the Seaforth Highlanders, who early this century had been lined-up on the banks of the River Spey for inspection by the Inspector General of the Volunteers. When the General arrived he immediately asked the Commanding Officer to form the men into a 'hollow square' so that he could speak to them. This was beyond the knowledge of drill possessed by Colonel McKessock, a legendary regimental figure, but he spoke the same language as his soldiers and gave the command, 'Roond me boys in a boorach with your 'erses' to the Spey'. Truly a command unmistakable even to an Englishman in the ranks!

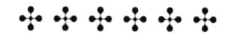

✣ ✣ ✣ ✣ ✣ ✣

Mrs V Robinson – Fillongley
Former ATS 536 Battery C Section 536(m)
HAA RA AA Command

LEADING LADIES

At the beginning of 1942, our gunsite was at Stockton-on-Tees. Mixed batteries were still a new project and some of the male NCOs were finding it hard to adapt to the changes and consequently it's fair to say we had a bit of a rough ride at first. As soldiers though, we accepted things without question and it certainly didn't do us any harm to be treated exactly the same as the male gunners. We learned very quickly where, as ATS, we could go and of course the one place we could NOT go: male quarters were strictly out of bounds!

One day at 2 pm changeover parade, the Command Post

teams and Gun teams marched away. The guard was changed and personnel on 24-Hour-Pass were dismissed. Two of us were designated Fire Piquet for the next 24 hours and were detailed to clean the male sergeant's accommodation before resuming normal Fire Piquet duties (such duties could involve all kinds of extra tasks - and usually did!)

Without saying a word, we 'fell-out' to collect the necessary equipment and it wasn't until we were out of sight of the Orderly Sergeant that we spoke. You can imagine some of the things we said then! We donned 'fatigues' and prepared to enter forbidden territory.

The hut was in desperate need of a spring clean and so we set about washing whisker-encrusted shaving mugs and making beds - we assumed the sergeants did not have to 'barrack' beds as we did. After a good while, we agreed we had done our best and were just about to leave when I had a plan....

It wasn't long before my companion joined me in apple-pieing each bed and sewing-up every pyjama leg (it was winter). We didn't want to go too far in fear of retribution in the form of the glasshouse, but after a particularly worrying night, nothing more came of the incident. Funnily enough, the ATS were never given that particular fatigue again - I wonder why!

✤ ✤ ✤ ✤ ✤ ✤

DHOBI DIVE

1944 found the Battery encamped on Romney Marsh - in the heart of Doodlebug Alley - part of the dive-bomber belt along the South Coast. As its name suggests, the site was marshy and so the slit trenches dug hither and thither about the place to provide emergency cover for those not manning the Guns or in the Command Post were often filled with water. I don't remember anyone ever jumping into the trenches but FALLING into them is another matter entirely!

On one memorable occasion, our laundry had just been delivered to the front entrance of camp. Before long, a male gunner was detailed to distribute the clean shirts to the respective owners and as he struggled with the bundles which were tied together with only the flimsiest piece of string, the inevitable happened! Down he went - and with him most of our shirts. The laundry was scattered everywhere and, being too interested in the state of our long-awaited clothes, nobody saw the hilarity of the occasion. Not surprisingly, we do now!

✢ ✢ ✢ ✢ ✢ ✢

Sir Harry Secombe CBE - London

IDIOT ON PARADE

Someone said to me recently - on Remembrance Sunday of all days - "Did you have a good war?" I was appalled, secretly, although I made self-deprecating noises at the time. "How can anyone apart from Mr Krupp have had a good war?" I thought. Yet I must confess that I'm the first one to try to teach our three grandchildren how to march whenever there's a military band on the box. I've given up trying to teach the wife - she was a toolsetter in the war anyway. There's a joke in there somewhere I think!

At regimental reunions, I'm there with the lads, stirring-up old memories. "Ere - d'you remember old Okehampton being caught with the ATS Sergeant-Major and saying he didn't mind jankers because he'd just realised his life's ambition?" - We'd then remember that Okehampton's real name was Woodcock!

It is amazing what the mind can be persuaded to forget, especially when reminiscing soldiers get together. Skirmishes become full scale battles, retreats turn into strategic withdrawals, mole hills become mountains - and when they've finished talking about sex they got onto the war.

I can't honestly say that I loved the war. I was in it but not of it you might say, and yet even at this distance I remember parts of it with a startling clarity and a certain rueful affection...

We were about to start on the invasion of Sicily and our regiment stood to attention on a sandy parade ground outside Sousse in Tunisia. Montgomery drove his desert-camouflaged staff car into the middle of the parade.

"Bweak wanks and gather wound", he said waving his fly whisk.

I was pushed along from behind, finishing up right against the car and directly beneath the great man himself who now began to address us.

"Take your hats off, I want to see what you look like."

I struggled to take off my beret, hot with the knowledge that beneath it lay four months' growth of wiry welsh hair. It had gone reasonably unnoticed within the fairly lax discipline of a unit actively engaged in battle, but old hawkeye above me was not going to miss it. To add to the general decrepit nature of my appearance, I was wearing a pair of steel spectacles which had been repaired at the bridge and at both sides with electrician's tape with the result that the frames sat on my nose at an angle of forty-five degrees. To complete my Hammer Horror kit, I was also wearing a piece of plaster over a mosquito bite on my chin. My hair, released from its bereted bondage, cascaded over my face and ears in a shower of sand.

Above me, Monty was telling us that we of the First Army were now joining the glorious Eighth Army and we had a tradition to keep up. Cautiously I raised my head and looked-up at him, trying to look committed to the task ahead.

"We're going to hit the Hun for six," he said - slapping his thigh with his fly whisk. I nodded fervently. The movement seemed to catch his eye and he looked down at me. What he saw seemed to strike him speechless and we stood looking at each other, locked in a moment of time, the two opposite ends of the scale face to face: a glittering Goliath and a dishevelled David, but both on the same side.

I cleared my throat, anxious to break the silence. "We're with you, Sir," I said fatuously. He shook his head slightly as if awakening from a petit mal, looked away and carried-on with his pep talk. But the pep seemed to have gone out of him and soon, with one last unbelieving glance in my direction, he was driven away wearing the expression of a man with something on his mind. He must have been reminded of Wellington's remark when watching a march past of his men - "I don't know what effect these men have upon the enemy, but, by God they terrify me."

✣ ✣ ✣ ✣ ✣ ✣

During my six and a half years in the army, the only other celebrities I managed to get near to were Spike Milligan who, like myself at that time was playing walk-on parts in battles; General Alexander who was playing the lead in the Mediterranean Theatre of War and Randolph Churchill whom Sergeant Ferris and myself captured outside Medjaz-el-Bab. He happened to be facing the wrong way at the time and his paratroop helmet did look teutonic in the half-light, and besides, who could believe a German who claimed to be Winston Churchill's son?

✣ ✣ ✣ ✣ ✣ ✣

There was the time when our twenty-five pounder clattered into a little town in southern Italy. We were the first Allied troops the inhabitants had seen and I sat astride my battered Matchless 350cc motor-bike like a miniature mechanised John Wayne. The townsfolk stood either side of the dusty main road waving hastily made Union Jacks and showering us with fruit and flowers from their balconies. The lads in the open trucks were upto their ears in grapes and figs, but I found it difficult to catch anything without letting go of the handlebars. I slowed to a halt, pretending to wave on the traffic.

"Frutta?", I enquired of a buxom signorina leaning from the first floor window.

"Si," she said, and knocked me off my bike with a well-aimed pomegranate!

✢ ✢ ✢ ✢ ✢ ✢

Ah, but life was not all like that. There was one little bit of glory which came my way, though perhaps not the way I expected.

After the fall of Tunis, a Victory Parade was held in which our regiment took part, and having been dismissed as too scruffy for the march past, I climbed up one of the palm trees lining the route. It was quite near the saluting base, and as there were a couple of cine cameras pointing my way, I tried to wriggle into a position where I could be seen.

My movements disturbed a colony of ants living among the leaves and I was too occupied trying to stop them marching up my shorts to pay much attention to the marching below, or the newsreel cameras. I wrote home to my parents in my weekly air mail letter that I might be seen on the screen if they looked for a palm tree near the saluting stand. After about three months solid cinema-going my mother saw me - well not all of me - just my left leg. She wrote to say that she was sure it was mine because the stocking was around the ankle and that's how mine always was when I was a boy, and did I get the balaclava helmet and the talcum powder?

I never got round to seeing it myself, despite watching 'All Our Yesterdays' on television with avid regularity. I wanted to point to the screen and say to my kids; "Look that's my left leg in Tunis." There's not much chance of that now though. Pity - I had a good-looking leg in those days!

✣ ✣ ✣ ✣ ✣ ✣

Major F S G Shore MC CdeG RA(Retd) - Long Ashton

SHOW PARADE

Early in 1948, when British troops were leaving Palestine for the Jews and Arabs to squabble over, the powers that be set-up a very patrician little army to effect a reasonably peaceful withdrawal from Galilee and all northern Palestine. This army was called CRAFORCE lead by Brigadier Ted Coloqhuon - Commander Royal Artillery, 6 Airborne Division.

As his Brigade Major, it was my duty to exercise his sway over those units under his charge: the 1st Guards Para Battalion; the 1st Battalion The Irish Guards and the 4/7th Royal Dragoon Guards.

In the last few days before pulling out of Galilee proper, the CRA and I drove a couple of jeeps into the hills to Safad from Rosh Pinna. We had planned to visit the Guards detachment there to show the flag as it were, but as we approached the hill-top, the excitement proved a little too much for the locals of both persuasions. Arab and Jew alike happily opened-fire in our general direction with - it seemed - whatever weapon they could lay their hands on. Since there was a distinct possibility that a stray shot might come a little too close for comfort, the CRA felt it prudent to take some ever-so-gentlemanly evasive action: it would never do to let the locals think we were scared!

Abandoning the jeeps outside a solitary house with an Irish Guards badge on it, we ambled slowly in - only to be met by a shattering crash! There in the centre of the room which occupied the whole of the first floor was an extremely large table. On its surface lay a selection of ladles, cooking-pots, enormous choppers of all shapes and sizes and an array of kitchen forks and rolling pins - all sparkling clean.

Behind the table, recovering from the springing-to-attention-with-foot-stamping which had set the house rocking, stood a Mick of gigantium proportions - bare-headed but not at a loss for protocol. His bellow once again set the crocks rattling and the windows bulging... "COOKING UTENSILS ... READY FOR INSPECTION ...SORRRRRRR!"

✥ ✥ ✥ ✥ ✥ ✥

NOW YOU SEE IT...NOW YOU DON'T

Towards the end of 1952, my battery was in direct support of the 1st Battalion The Black Watch near the notorious Hook feature in Korea. One morning after a particularly nasty ding-dong with the Chinese enemy (thinly disguised as North Koreans), the sun rose to unveil a scene more devastating than could be imagined; the Officers' loo was lying in tatters on the frozen ground! It had been a sort of sacking-cum-sandbag erection around an old-fashioned thunder-box and had stood proud in the middle of an open space not far from the Officers' Mess dug-out.

As he marched upto me to report this disaster, my splendid BSM - a dour Highland Scot - produced the wonderfully graphic wording which has since become almost legendary. "Och. Sorr, them Gooks have been very obstreperous the night. Ye have no loo the noo!"

✥ ✥ ✥ ✥ ✥ ✥

MOBILE RELIEF

Towards the end of the war in Korea, one of my men was being held in the much-feared Canadian 'stockade' pending court's-martial. Quite miraculously he managed to escape - only to resurface again some weeks later near Inchon in splendidly bizarre circumstances.

Apparently he had managed to pinch an American 10-ton-type lorry; begged, borrowed or stolen a lot of old scrap timber and sacking; converted the back of the lorry into four booths (complete with one bunk each!); coerced several local girls to join him (without much difficulty it seemed!) and was busily running a highly profitable mobile brothel. Now that's initiative for you!

✥ ✥ ✥ ✥ ✥ ✥

D I A Smith Esq - Wickham

BULL'S BEADLE'S BUNNIES

I hadn't been in the regiment long, when Bull's Troop was tasked to assist the much-maligned TV celebrity Jeremy Beadle with the opening footage of his new television show. The filming was designed to show a number of bunny rabbits arriving at the studio having undertaken a sequence of fearless activities akin to freefall parachuting and abseiling. It was here that the Gentlemen of Bull's were asked to assist.

Understandably, the parachuting Bunnies of Bull's came in for a lot of stick and leg-pulling from other members of the regiment - and - not surprisingly, from the rest of the Airborne Brigade in the bars and clubs of Aldershot. The abseiling was harmless and rather uneventful, but back at Lille Barracks things were hotting-up.

Beadle is renowned for being a bit of a practical joker and during the filming of the bunny escapade, he had parked his rather nice car near the square. As a lowly and very-very new 'nig-subbie' I was not aware of the considerable amount of fork-lift truck traffic which was passing my office window; (I say my office window - of course at that time I didn't even have a chair of my own - let alone an office!). Backward and forward they went. Simulated-ammo pallets were followed by packages of all sorts balanced precariously on the forks. At one point, I'm sure the Master Chef's Cortina went past - (that bit could be apocryphal) -but even that didn't have any impact on me. They were, after all, trained soldiers and were no doubt involved in some form of internal security operation instigated by 'Biff' the no-nonsense RSM at the time.

Shortly before lunch, the bunnies returned to barracks. Ten minutes after hopping through the main gate - with Beadle no doubt secreted among the throng, an almighty cheer erupted from the square - in fact from the vicinity of the Beadle-mobile

I looked-out of the office window and in the middle of what must have been the whole of the regiment stood a very bemused and no-doubt concerned TV personality.

In his absence, the remaining men of Bull's and various other hoods had moved everything fork-liftable from its usual resting place and planted it deftly around the most expensive car in camp. By the time Beadle had found his car keys and prepared to set-off back to TV-land, his car was hidden behind several storeys of seemingly unmovable army material.

In all fairness he did take it quite well and before leaving camp, gave an impromptu display of card tricks -quickly confusing at least one gunner by shuffling an invisible pack of cards and relating it to his first sexual experience!

✤ ✤ ✤ ✤ ✤ ✤

R Thomas Esq - Lee-on-Solent

MEMORIES OF AN RSM BY A LOWLY GUNNER

It was Autumn 1954. There we were at Woolwich waiting for our move to join 94th Locating Regiment in Munsterlager when the news was broken that our escort for the journey would be none other than our new RSM.

WO1(RSM) Harding got us all on parade and in no uncertain terms explained who was to be the boss for our journey. After a brief but thorough inspection of his new charges, the RSM marched us to Woolwich Station loaded-down with our worldly possessions.

My first personal encounter with the RSM was at the 'Tube' station waiting for the train to Liverpool Street. As the train pulled-in, I picked-up my kit bag and balancing it on top of my back pack suddenly and uncontrollably lunged forward. Someone had pushed me in the back. Spouting out a flurry of expletives, I looked around for the culprit to give him a more permanent indication of my displeasure when what should I see but a red emblazoned arm withdrawing from the vicinity of my back. Needless to say, I was asked in true RSM fashion to refrain from swearing in public...but the damage was done - I was now a marked man! The remainder of the journey to Munsterlager was understandably a little subdued. Not surprisingly I opted to keep my head down and hoped the RSM would somehow forget my name. FAT CHANCE!

Once in barracks I was appointed to the MT Office. The lads were a good bunch and I couldn't help thinking that things were already looking up. But things weren't what they seemed. Horror of horrors - who should have his office opposite the MT but a certain WO1(RSM) Harding! - a feeling of abject horror descended on my newly found world. Actually, it soon became clear that RSM Harding was in fact a very fair man and if you ever got on the wrong side of him, you probably deserved it. But from the perspective of a young Gunner it was perhaps safer to keep as much distance from such a senior hand as was at all possible!

The weeks passed by and things were going just fine. I had managed to avoid incurring the wrath of the man himself for some time. But a chance discovery of an old parachutist's bike in the MT store served to rock this period of relative equilibrium. The bike had been left in a bad way and was in need of some basic servicing. Who better to exercise his initiative to get it back on the road, than your's truly?

After the necessary maintenance I was, for the next few days, the envy of the camp having something other than Shank's pony to get from place to place. But Thomas had done it again. I was informed in no uncertain terms by Sergeant Coughlin - my MT boss - that it would be in my best interest to return the bike to the store. Not surprisingly I wasn't going down without a fight. "But Sarge.." pleaded this hapless gunner, "I repaired it..Nobody else was using it..After all, it doesn't belong to anyone.." Sadly I was wrong. The bike did in fact belong to someone and as luck would have it, that someone just happened to be one WO1(RSM) Harding! Once again I spent the next few weeks keeping my head down whenever the RSM was around but bikes seemed to have an uncanny habit of landing me right in it with the RSM.

Winter had arrived at Munsterlager and with it a good covering of snow. The train journey from Woolwich seemed an age away. I was by now considered an 'old hand' and given the privilege of wearing my civilian clothing when not on duty. One Sunday lunchtime I was returning from the cookhouse with a bunch of friends when the crisp silence was broken by a strange hissing sound coming from behind. We turned to investigate from where this sound was coming, and who else should we see perched on his new bike (not the parachutists's I hasten to add!), but the RSM battling against the elements on his way to the Sergeants' Mess. As he came parallel to us I politely said, "Good morning Sir", but instead of returning my compliment, the RSM just looked at me aghast and promptly fell from his mount.

He quickly and smartly regained his composure and recovered himself before proceeding with his journey. As soon as he was out of sight, my companions turned to me and enquired what I had done to upset the RSM this time - I was genuinely unsure - I simply didn't know.

The following morning though I was greeted by an irate Sergeant Coughlin who informed me that I was to be outside the RSM'S office at 11 o'clock. "But Sarge," I begged, "what have I done this time?"

"You know ****** **** what you've done" retorted my boss. "Don't you ever wear that ******* ***** zoot suit of yours around camp again - the RSM hates them."

The penny dropped. In the days before I joined-up I had been a teddy boy and the only suit I owned happened to be a rather natty set of drapes - apparently it was the sight of my drain pipe trousers which had caused the RSM to fall from his bike!

✤ ✤ ✤ ✤ ✤ ✤

General Sir Harry Tuzo GCB OBE MC DL MA - Fakenham.

A DOUBLE-EDGED INTRODUCTION

During my first Guest Night at 5 RHA having been in the Horse Artillery only 3 days, a gigantic and rather senior officer leapt on my back for a game of High Cocklerum....

....10 days later I was released from Tidworth Hospital with my leg still encased in a plaster cast - the metal shoe of which continually seemed to be wearing-out. My initiative bore fruit however, and I eventually evolved an excellent system whereby I could be shod by the Battery Fitters while standing on one leg...they did of course have to use the blow lamp with extreme caution!

A week after my return to Regimental Duty, I was enjoying a curry lunch in the Mess when I had cause to tactfully eject a hard object from my mouth. The object turned out to be a human tooth - not mine I might add - complete with roots.

My introduction to Gunner life was developing into quite a unique experience and I couldn't help but wonder if someone was trying to tell me something!

P Viggars Esq MP – Westminster/Gosport.

TROUBLESOME TERRIER

A huge Royal Artillery display was scheduled at Wembley Stadium one evening. All the equipment was drawn-up in gleaming serried ranks. The stand was packed; the Honorary Colonel, Admiral of the Fleet Earl Mountbatten arrived; all was ready for the start. A gun was fired to open the event; the Regimental Band played the National Anthem, the whole stadium rose to attention, every officer saluted - except one.

The Territorial Officer was a bright chap but perhaps not the most military of men. As the spotlight illuminated the arena, there he was, strolling before the stand, hands in pockets, pipe in mouth and not a care in the world. Mountbatten was appalled and when the officer in question was called to explain his conduct, the excuse was perhaps more disconcerting than the crime. "Well Sir," said the hapless officer, "I'm awfully sorry, but I did not recognise the tune."

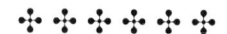

✢ ✢ ✢ ✢ ✢ ✢

Colonel D Walton CBE MC TD MA - Matlock.

DIGNITY

"Some are born great, some achieve greatness and some have greatness thrust upon them."

If this applies in my case, it is the third. It started when I was "spare wanking" as Assistant Section Commander, (can you get any lower?) for a troop of 5.5" Gun Hows of 58th (Suffolk) Medium Regiment.

We were at Fondouk Gap in April 1943. I never liked gun positions - noisy and over-run with competent people who knew about buffers, recuperators and snifting valves. So when the cry "spare wank to the tannoy" reverberated around the site, I was amazed that anyone wanted to speak to me. It was the Assistant Command Post Officer - also a subaltern - called John Neal of later fame but glorying then in the power of a real job.

"The Troop Commander - Donald Moffat - has just had an unfortunate encounter with a mortar splinter at the OP end and is no more. The BC's ordered me to send someone responsible to take over. The trouble is, there is no one responsible; there is only you."

So off I dashed wandering what I would find. I vaguely remembered some useless information that one did an inventory on such occasions, but by the time I had arrived, the OP Party had done this already. Reading through the list, I spotted a half bottle of whisky and suggested we reduce our load by putting this to good use, but was informed by Lance-Bombardier McNally, the OP Ack, that this had already been designated for medicinal purposes.

I then reported to the Commanding Officer of the Guards Battalion I had to support (Coldstream, I think). He was singularly uninterested in me, or anything else for that matter. It appeared we were moving from ridge to ridge, so I applied common sense, remained within call and dodged along from bush to bush to take what cover I could find. This soon got quite tiring and I noted that the Battalion Commander was walking, hands behind his back, looking at the ground. To add to this apparent scene of nonchalance, his guardsmen, rather than taking evasive action were moving from ridge to ridge at the high port, their Barrack Dress trousers immaculately pressed. Such an approach seemed to work for them, so taking a leaf from their book, I smartly fell-in four paces behind the Colonel and did likewise.

Next day, there were two further ridges to take. For some reason an anti-aircraft captain joined us to give further support. I was a day senior in close quarter fighting, so even as a subaltern, he placed himself under my orders - the Battalion Commander clearly not wanting to talk to either of us. As we continued our advance, the new arrival immediately started darting between bushes - presumably taking advantage of what little cover there was. After an hour of this, he very smartly fell-in behind saying, "My goodness, you've really taught me a lesson." "Think nothing of it," I said, "just comes with experience!"

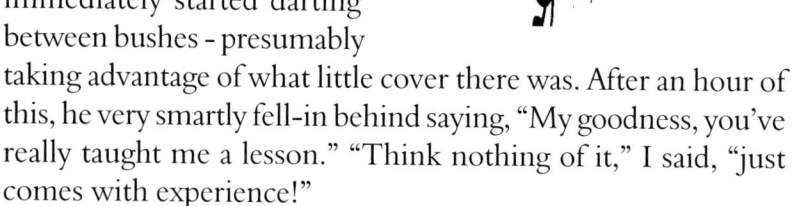

I really loved the work as an Observation Officer. There was nobody shouting at you, lots of wide open spaces and ample time to study nature. Jerry occasionally made things a little unfriendly but as no-one else wanted the job, I took it with gratitude. No more snifting valves and spare wanking for me - thanks John!

DECISIONS-DECISIONS

"Shall I shoot them, Sir?"

Bombardier Hill was preparing to take-on at least 10,000 Huns who were fast approaching my OP party and our armoured car. It was May 1943 and we were clearly visible on the Tunis to Nabeul road - near what is now called Hammamet. I had been ordered to make a mad dash to find 6th Armoured Division who were hoping to cut Jerry off in the Emtidaville Hills before he reached possible safety in the Cap Bon Peninsula. My final orders from the BC were quite succinct; "What are you waiting for, Dennis?"

As I purveyed the field grey flood coming across the open plain from the hill, quite what order to give Bombardier Hill I was unsure. Our 5.5 Gun Howitzers were way behind us and all I had in the armoured car was a machine gun and our rifles. We could perhaps account for a hundred before we were swamped, so as they closed purposely on us, I decided to wait on events showing a nonchalance I didn't feel. "Point our gun in the air, Bombardier." As they got to within fifty yards, not a shot had been fired by us or indeed at us and it wasn't long before I could see their faces - smiling and obviously very happy. Things started to fit together when the radio crackled into life and the news came through that von Arnim had just accepted - albeit reluctantly - an unconditional surrender. The hordes trotted on and passed us like good boy scouts and I readily indicated the way back to Tunis - and to

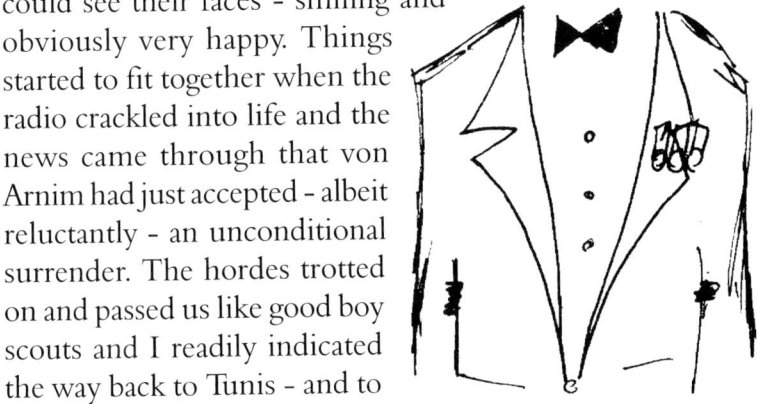

Canada. The flow of prisoners was never-ending. Altogether 250,000 surrendered in Tunisia of which 10,000 were claimed by my party of four - singularly the largest number to surrender to a subaltern in either world war.

As we pulled-over into a shaded cutting to have some sandwiches, both sides of the road were packed with Jerries. Suddenly, as one, they all rose to their feet and braced-up to attention as a scout car drove past us into captivity. "Wer ist das?", I asked eloquently of a Hun neighbour. "General von Arnim", came the reply. I got up too!

✣ ✣ ✣ ✣ ✣ ✣

THE GUNNER HERITAGE APPEAL

The Royal Artillery is currently raising funds to build a new, yet dignified National Museum of Artillery by the River Thames at Woolwich in the Royal Arsenal.

The museum will tell the story of Artillery in the British Army since its first use at Crecy in 1346 to its vital role in present day world affairs. A technical, historical and artistic account of gunnery, it will also be a show-piece to display the treasures and riches of the Regiment - including its 62 Victoria Crosses.

The project is challenging but considerable progress has already been made by Gunners - serving and retired and there is no doubt that the end result will be something of which Gunners everywhere will be very proud.

Having purchased this book, you have already contributed to the Gunner Heritage Appeal which is coordinating the fund-raising for the museum and for that, many thanks. Should you wish further information about the appeal or would like to make an additional donation, please contact: The Chief Executive, Gunner Heritage Appeal Royal Artillery Barracks Woolwich SE18 4 BH

✣ ✣ ✣ ✣ ✣ ✣

HAVE YOU A TALE TO TELL?

Whenever Gunners gather together, the air is thick with stories similar - although not necessarily as clean as - those you have just read. If you have had any connection with the Royal Regiment, you no doubt have your own memories of the lighter side of Gunner life - memories worth sharing. It is planned to compile another collection of "Egg Banjos" to benefit the Heritage Appeal. Should you wish to share your own Gunner tales and boost the fund further, please send them to:

Duncan Smith c/o HOMESTEAD PUBLICATIONS West Cottage, Top Street, Pilton, Somerset BA4 4DF.
Many thanks.

✥ ✥ ✥ ✥ ✥ ✥